PETER HOWOR

EAST YORKSHIRE CRICKET
1778-1914

LOWNDES PUBLICATIONS
17 LOWNDES PARK
DRIFFIELD
(01377 253768)

Published 1995

Lowndes Publications (Driffield)
17 Lowndes Park,
Driffield,
YO25 7BE,
(01377 253768)

Copyright Peter Howorth 1995

ISBN 0 9517630 2 4

British Library Cataloguing-in-Publication Data.
A catalogue record for this book is available
from the British Library.

Printed by
Clifford Ward & Co. (Bridlington) Ltd.,
55 West Street, Bridlington,
East Yorkshire, YO15 3DZ.

CONTENTS

Page

ACKNOWLEDGEMENTS

The published sources for this book are indicated in footnotes at the end of each chapter. The files of local newspapers are scattered around the East and North Ridings, but I am grateful to the staff of Humberside Libraries for their help, especially at Hull and Beverley. The staff at Driffield Library have been helpful in obtaining British Library material for me. As always the staff of the *Driffield Times* have accepted my frequent visits with good nature.

I owe a debt of gratitude to a number of individuals and clubs for helping with information or photographs. They are, (in no particular order):

Mr. Peter Milne of Londesborough Park C.C., Bridlington C.C. and the late Mr. J. Wood, Mr. Mike Rhodes of Hornsea C.C., Mr. Mike Hutchinson and Beverley C.C., the Sykes Lodge, Driffield, Mr. J. Lonsdale, Mr. M. Lonsdale, Mr. Norris, Mr. G. Southwell, Mr. M. Fearn, Mr. M. Craven, Mrs. P. M. Cureton, Mr. B. Nattriss, Mr. Keith Savage, Mr. G. Beswick, Mr. Sam Calvert, Mr. T. Green, Mrs. W. Taylor, Mr. M. Hammond and Mr. David Wells.

A special word of thanks is owed to Mr. Norman Wilson.

The photo of cricket on Beverley Westwood is part of the Humberside Library collection and is reproduced by the permission of Humberside Leisure Services.

LIST OF ILLUSTRATIONS

LIST OF ILLUSTRATIONS

THE EARLY DAYS

In September 1824, 15 men of the Beverley Club travelled to play against 15 men of the Doncaster Club on the race ground. Given the time of the year and the difficulty of the journey, it seems probable that they combined the game with a visit to the races. They 'played cleverly' to win that game. At the end of the first day they were left needing 8 to win with '6 wickets to go down' but the game was 'left off in consequence of being too dark' and was 'played out the following morning'. Beverley lost the return fixture on the Westwood.

Next season the *Yorkshire Gazette* announced:

'A grand match will be played on Tuesday 30th (of August 1825) upon the Beverley Cricket ground between the Gentlemen of Beverley (or East Riding) and the Doncaster clubs. As the above clubs have played twice before and each claimed the victory, this match is expected to excite the greatest interest among the amateurs of the noble game and should the weather be favourable the ground will be numerously and fashionably attended.'

The score-card for that match, containing an all-run 6, is interesting for the way it is set out.

ELEVEN OF BEVERLEY v ELEVEN OF DONCASTER
Played on The Westwood, 30th August, 1825

BEVERLEY:		1st Innings		
Sticker	How Out	By Whom	Notches	Total
G. Kelley	c	R. Cooke	1212	6
A. Maister	b	Markham	11121	7
Stanley	c	Wharton	1132	7
Worsley	b	Wharton		0
Broadhead	b	Wharton	122	5
G. Legard	b	Wharton	11311	7

BEVERLEY: 1st Innings

Sticker	How Out	By Whom	Notches	Total
J. Blanchard	b	Wharton	1	1
Strachey	b	Markham	1	1
Foulis	b	Markham	2	2
Fawkes	b	Markham	2	2
Hutton (for Bower .. late)	not out			0
Byes			21	3
				40

DONCASTER: 1st Innings

Sticker	How Out	By Whom	Notches	Total
Armitage	b	Worsley	12	3
Lascelles	b	Bower	2123212132 1112211122	33
Markham	hit his wicket			0
Coulman	b	Broadhead	3133	10
Wharton	b	Broadhead		0
G. Cooke	b	Broadhead		0
Dennison	b	Broadhead		0
Cator	before his wicket		22121121	12
R. Cooke	b	Broadhead	11	2
Sir W. Cooke	before his wicket		21	3
Jackson	not			0
Byes			111	3
				67

BEVERLEY: 2nd Innings

Sticker	How Out	By Whom	Notches	Total
Kelley	b	Markham	31161311313	24
Maister	c	Jackson		0
Stanley	b	Markham		0
Bower	b	Markham	1	1
Broadhead	run out		1	1
Legard	c	Sir W. Cooke	111	3
Worsley	c	Wharton		0
Blanchard	b	Wharton	112211321211	18
Strachey	c	Wharton	2211	6

8

Sticker	How Out	By Whom	Notches	Total
Foulis	not out		111	3
Fawkes	b	Wharton	21	3
Byes			31111	7
				34

DONCASTER: 2nd Innings

Sticker	How Out	By Whom	Notches	Total
Lascelles	b	Broadhead	1112122112	14
Jackson	b	Broadhead	111	3
Armitage	b	Broadhead		0
Wharton	not out		111412	10
G. Cooke	not out			0
Byes			31111	7
				34

Doncaster won by 7 wickets

The return match that season was played on Doncaster Race Course on 17th October.

Cricket was enormously popular in Yorkshire in the 1820's, particularly in the Sheffield area where some very competitive matches attracted large crowds. George Steer opened his New Ground at Darnall Hall in 1824 after the collapse of a temporary grandstand at the old ground had injured a number of people. He attracted 20,000 spectators to the second day of a match between the All England Club and 22 of Yorkshire in 1825 and this was by no means the largest gate.

The game could not attract such numbers in the East Riding, but cricket was being played on an organised basis from an early date. The earliest record is of a match in 1778.

'On Thursday, August 13th at Wallingfen near North Cave, Howden beat Beverley by 64 notches, for 50 guineas. Play began at 12.00. The first innings, Beverley got 48 notches, Howden 42 : second innings Beverley 26 and Howden 96.'

The two sides played the return game the following month, again at Wallingfen, which may have been at a convenient distance for both clubs.

'On Thursday September 10th was played on Wallingfen,

9

the last great Cricket Match of the season between the Gentlemen of Beverley and of Howden for 50 guineas, which was won with great ease by Beverley. Wickets were pitched at 12.00. 1st innings, Beverley (tho' very unlucky) got 59 notches, Howden 39 : second innings Howden 69 which was run off by Beverley, who had four hands to come in.'[1]

There is nothing in these reports to suggest that cricket was a new venture in the area, indeed the reference to 'the last great Cricket Match of the season' points to these being only two of a number of games that had been played. Both clubs predate the York Club formed in 1784. Howden is quite close to the heartland of early Yorkshire cricket and the game is likely to have spread there from South Yorkshire. The Club was clearly established on a firm footing and was still in existence in 1788.

'Lately were played two cricket matches, one at Howden and the other at Wallingfen, by the gentlemen of the cricket club established at Howden and the gentlemen farmers of Saltmarsh and Wallingfen.'

The farmers won both games 'with great ease' against the expectations of the bookmakers who were offering odds of 5 and 6 to 1 against them.[2] They played against Selby in 1800 when they were again the favourites, starting at 7 to 1, but when they went 20 runs behind on the first innings, the odds shortened to evens and then swung to 7 to 1 on Selby, who 'won with great ease'.[3]

Beverley in the second half of the 18th Century was a centre for the gentry of the East Riding. They were drawn there by the Quarter Sessions, the Assembly Rooms and the Race Course. A network of turnpike roads gave good communications with the rest of the Riding and many of the landed gentry had town houses in the borough. It is hardly surprising if a cricket club formed part of their social activities. It may well be that for very different reasons, Howden and Beverley were the earliest centres of cricket in the Riding.

The first score-card for an East Riding match is for one played in Hull in 1798 between '11 Officers of the 4th and 5th West Yorkshire Regiments and 10 Officers of Regiments Encamped in Holderness.' The date is in the middle of the French Wars when the War Office took the threat of a French invasion through Holderness extremely seriously. There were large numbers of troops in the area and it is perhaps significant that two of the regiments involved in the

10

match were from the West Riding. They may very well have helped to popularise the game around Hull. Since the match was 'played at the cricket ground in this town' it suggests that there was at least one club playing in the city before 1798.

Two of the players involved in that game were Major-General Lennox and Sir Charles Turner, who had become the M.P. for Hull in 1796. They organised a much more ambitious two-day game for 100 guineas a side at the end of the season. The match was played on Beverley Westwood in September, between Lennox (now promoted to Lt.-General) with 10 Nottinghamshire players and Turner's side of 11 players of Yorkshire 'out of different clubs'. Since none of the sources for this match give a score-card, it is impossible to know if the Nottinghamshire side was drawn from a militia regiment stationed in the area or was drawn from the powerful Nottingham clubs. That the game was played on the Westwood, surely suggests that the Beverley club was still in existence at that date and it seems likely that Turner, a Hull M.P., would have at least a nucleus of East Riding players 'out of different clubs'. The match incidentally was won by Nottinghamshire who scored 46 and 104 against Yorkshire's 48 and 97. It was not, of course, a county match in any meaningful sense of the term.

There can be no certainty that the Beverley club of the 1770's was the same club that played fifty years later in 1824 and 1825 against Doncaster. Those teams were members of the strong Beverley and East Riding Club, powerful enough to challenge any of the clubs in the North. It looks as if they toured Lincolnshire in 1829 when three Beverley players made up the side for the Norfolk Club in their match against Louth, who were believed at that time to be 'fully equal to any provincial club in the kingdom'. Louth's supremacy was confirmed in 1832 when they were triumphant over Southwell in a series of games and 'they have also easily beaten the Norfolk, Beverley, Brigg and Horncastle clubs and may justly, as cricketers, be designated the first gentlemen's club in England'.[4]

Beverley's strength can be gauged from two matches played at Canterbury in 1839. These were a precursor of the 'Grand Cricket Week' or 'The Canterbury Week' which began in 1842 and which was one of the high points of the season. It was the Scarborough Festival of its time, attracting not only the most famous cricketers of the day, but drawing the aristocracy and the members of fashionable society in large numbers.[5] When Beverley played two

11

matches against a Kent side, Chilston Park, Felix and Alfred Mynn, two of the greatest players of that or any other time, made their first appearance at Canterbury. The first encounter 'being confined by arrangement to a day's play was left unfinished. The return also shared the same fate, although Beverley which had Mr. Felix for its given man, seemed on the occasion to be much the stronger side'.[6] A given man was often a form of handicapping to even out two sides and 'make a match' for a stake.

A speaker at the opening of Beverley's Norwood ground in 1909 claimed to have the score-book of the Beverley and E.R.C.C. from 1825 to 1844. The club was certainly in existence before 1825 and was offering a prize to be competed for by the junior clubs in the town in 1845. A lithograph exists by Henry Ward, of a match between the East Kent Club and Beverley at Canterbury on 4th August 1845, but it does seem likely that they played their last game soon afterwards and certainly before 1849. A group calling themselves the Old England Club, limited to players aged 50 or over, reconvened in Beverley every year in the 1850's and early 1860's to play a few matches on 'the old ground' on the Westwood. They appointed a management committee to supervise arrangements, drew up a code of behaviour and paid 1/- each towards expenses. Judged by the respectful tones in which their games were reported and the references to past glories, the Old England Club may well have been the last vestiges of the Beverley and E.R.C.C.

Club cricket seems to have been slower to develop on the Wolds, though there is every reason to suppose that the game was played there from an early date. There is a marked similarity between the Wolds and the Downs, the area which dominated cricket in the late 18th Century. The close cropped sheep walks, covered in a fine carpet down of grass, were ideal for cricket and just the sort of environment that cricket historians have linked to the development of the game in the south of England. One writer, recalling his early 19th Century boyhood in a Wold's village, wrote 'On the Wold, nearly opposite my father's house, the young men and boys of the village played at cricket almost every Sunday in fine weather'.[7] Such knock-about games must have been part of the fabric of village life throughout much of the 18th Century. It should perhaps not be forgotten that Squire Osbaldeston, one of the larger than life figures who shaped early 19th Century cricket, had his estates at Hutton Buscel on the edge of the Wolds and was closely related to the

Mitford's of Hunmanby. It was the notorious 'Squire George' who took part with William Lambert in a single wicket match for 50 guineas against the equally unsavoury cleric, Lord Frederick Beauclerk and T. C. Howard. When Osbaldeston fell ill, Beauclerk refused to postpone the game and invoked the 'play or pay' rule. Osbaldeston then insisted that his partner, William Lambert, took on both opponents, which he did, dismissing Howard and bowling wide after wide to Beauclerk, until he had completely lost his temper and was bowled by a straight one. Wides at that time were not penalised with a run. Perhaps Osbaldeston was introduced to cricket on the Wolds!

If the landscape of the Wolds resembled that of the Downs, nothing that even vaguely resembled the organised matches of the Hambledon Club at Broadhalfpenny Down was to be found on the Wolds at this date. The population was sparse and there was no body of men with the leisure time to play the game. In Nottingham and Sheffield where the game grew in popularity at the beginning of the 19th Century, the lace and cutlery workers were on piece work and time could, at a pinch, be found. The same could be said for the West Riding textile workers, at least until the mills replaced the domestic system, but for the farm workers of the East Riding no such opportunity existed. Knock-about games on a Sunday evening on the wold would be all the time that was available. It seems clear from other evidence that inter-village matches became common only at a later date. It was to need a change of fashion for the game to develop. As the popularity of fox-hunting overtook the previous favourite pastimes of fowling and fishing in the Hull valley, the Wolds came into their own.

'Our hounds are all healthy, our horses are sound.
O'er the Wolds we will show you the best of good ground'.

The increased demand for corn during the Napoleonic Wars led to the large scale enclosure of the Wolds, bringing new wealth to the landed families that chose to build their country houses there. This group had both the money and the leisure time to pursue their interests. A generation later, it was their sons who had learned the game at public school and at university, who were willing to partake in it with all and sundry and encouraged it on their estates.

There is another reason why information on the game is sparse before the Victorian period. The local market towns on the edge of

13

the Wolds, Beverley, Market Weighton, Driffield, Pocklington and Bridlington, had no local newspapers before, in the earliest case, the 1850's. The regional newspapers of York and Hull were not interested in and probably had no knowledge of, such rustic games that did take place. It needed the participation of the gentry to arouse enough interest for the game on the Wolds to be thought worth recording.

It is only then that enough information emerges to give a clear picture of the cricket scene on the Wolds. By that time the framework of the game had developed into a form that would be readily recognisable to a modern spectator. The length of the pitch, the height of the stumps and the weight of the ball had all been standardised. A third stump had been added and the normal length of the game had been established as two innings, though matches of three innings were still to be found in the early 19th Century. In 1812 Malton lost to Slingsby by 'one innings and a half' i.e. by an innings and 5 wickets in a three innings game. More specifically, in 1817 Kirkbymoorside beat Yarm in a 12-a-side match for 50 guineas, each team to bat three times.

Yarm scored $29 + 29 + 53 = 111$
Kirkbymoorside: $74 + 23 + 16$ for $2 = 113$[8]

Even as late as 1826, Hovingham played a three innings match against the combined Slingsby and Terrington Clubs. They won a close match, after which 'Slingsby and Terrington challenges to play Hovingham again for from £20 to £50 a side'.

The laws of the game had progressed to a point that would be readily understandable to our eyes and the quainter aspects of the early laws had been dropped. Thus, at the beginning of the 18th Century, batsmen completed a notch, or run, by touching the bat that was held by the umpire. This explains why in the paintings of the period, both umpires are shown standing by their respective wicket and not at square leg. A rule drawn up for a match in 1727 expressly stated 'The batt men for every one they count are to touch the umpire's stick'[9] while a poem describing a match in 1706 contains the lines:

'each at his wicket near at hand,
propped on his staff, the Umpires stand,
the runner's bat must touch their pale,
or else the run will nought avail'.[10]

14

After 1788 a batsman whose leg had stopped the ball from hitting the wicket could be out LBW whether or not the move had been deliberate and the law had gone that let a batsman charge down a fielder going for a catch.

The tactics of the game had also developed. In the 18th Century most bowlers bowled fast daisy-cutters, relying on the uneven pitch to beat the bat, but by the beginning of the 19th Century 'length' and 'lob' bowling were also common. The curved hockey stick bats that were perhaps best adapted to 'shooters' gave way to straight bats that encouraged batsmen to come down the pitch to under-arm lobs and 'give her the rush'. Round-arm bowling, usually tolerated from 1823, finally became legal in 1835 as long as the bowling arm was not above the shoulder. All these methods of bowling were to be found in this area well into the last decades of the 19th Century, indicating perhaps that old approaches retained their local popularity long after they had become old fashioned at Lords.

Sources:

[1]   *York Courant* August and September 1778. Quoted in G. B. Buckley *Fresh Light on 18th Century Cricket* 1935. Page 85.

[2]   G. B. Buckley. *Fresh Light on Pre-Victorian Cricket* 1937. Page 15.

[3]   E. S. Holmes. *History of Yorkshire County Cricket 1833-1903.* 1904. Page 13.

[4]   Buckley. Page 153.

[5]   There is a fictional, but highly entertaining, account of Canterbury Week in G. M. Fraser's *Flashman's Lady*, which gives an accurate account of the atmosphere and the cricket of the time.

[6]   Charles Box. *The English Game of Cricket* 1877. page 161.

[7]   J. R. Mortimer. *A Victorian Boyhood on the Wolds* East Yorkshire Local History Society 1978. Page 21.

[8]   Buckley. Page 91.

[9]   R. S. Rait Kerr. *The Laws of Cricket* 1950. Page 10.

[10]   William Goldwin. *A Cricket Match.* 1706. Translated from the Latin by H. A. Perry, 1922.

THE YEARS OF UNCERTAINTY

Cricket historians have identified a sharp decline in the number of matches recorded at the beginning of the 19th Century. In 1799 over the whole of the country, 60 games are known about, of which there are full score-cards for 27. By 1804 this has become 31 and 12. The figures only reach their former level at the end of the French Wars, remain constant into the 1820's and then steadily increase.[1] The situation in the East Riding does not fit easily into this national pattern.

Apart from a game between Old Ripon and Nottingham, no match of any kind was reported in the *Hull Advertiser*, the local paper with the best news coverage between 1798 and 1824. Were matches in the East Riding not being played or simply not being reported? It has been suggested that the need to cover the events of the French Wars from 1793 to 1815 drove cricket out of the papers and it is certainly true that in a city like Hull, the shipping movements in and out of the Humber and the serious impact of the wars on overseas trade occupied much of the available space, but there were long lulls in the war and even in the more serious times, the editor found space for the most mundane local trivia. Some have argued that the gentry were so fully occupied with raising and training the local militia that they had no time for cricket. This may be so, but the presence of large numbers of militia in the Holderness area, at least until the danger of a French invasion had ended, may well have contributed to the popularity of the sport in this area, as the 1798 matches perhaps show.

The *Yorkshire Gazette* provided excellent cover of the sports which interested early 19th Century society. Horse racing dominated its columns, but hunting, shooting, boxing, cock-fighting, even lion baiting by dogs on two occasions, were all faithfully recorded. Its cricket reporting is impressive and it is difficult to believe that many matches in the area went unmentioned. It is clear from their pages that in the 1820's, clubs were well established throughout the North and West Ridings, but with the exception of the Beverley-Doncaster matches of 1824-25, only two

East Riding games are recorded. Howden played Selby for 20 guineas at Barmby on the Marsh in 1820 and in September 1823 Beverley played Hull C.C. on the Westwood. This was a return match, 'the former was won by Beverley with 10 wickets to spare. On the present occasion the termination was still more decidedly in favour of Beverley', who won by an innings and 113 runs. 'Bets at starting 3 to 1 on winners; after Beverley's first innings 10 and 12 to 1; after Hull's first innings 100 to 1'.

There is circumstantial evidence that other games were being played but going unreported in the East Riding. At a York game on the Knavesmire in 1832 'several of the old club, who about thirty years ago, contested with some of the best clubs of the kingdom' were recognised. 'Thirty years ago' is too vague a term on which to build an argument, but whatever date the writer meant, the games were not reported. Stronger evidence is the score-book of the Beverley and East Riding C.C. from 1825 to 1844, which clearly implies matches being played. None of them was reported in the *Hull Advertiser* at a time when it had a regular Beverley correspondent supplying it with news from the town and when the paper could be as boastful of Yorkshire achievements as the most chauvinistic of Tykes could desire. There is a persistent, but unsubstantiated tradition that Londesborough Park played a match against Pocklington School in 1820, but there is no other reference to the club at that time. The lack of reporting on East Riding cricket is all the more puzzling because the paper carried news of a match between Grimsby and Lincoln and between Louth and the Norfolk Club in 1829.

The clearest evidence that cricket was being played but not being reported, is a fascinating document from Bridlington, 'The Bridlington Cricket Club Accounts and Rules' dated 1820.[2] The Society was formed on 1st June 1820 by seven gentlemen, the Rev. Arthur Strickland, who became President, George Hudson the Treasurer, John Harding the Secretary, Francis Metcalfe, John Strickland and Christopher and Thomas Soulsby. They obviously intended it to be an exclusive club. New members seeking admission had to face a ballot, 'one black ball to exclude'. There was a high subscription of 10/6d but in addition, 'members shall be answerable for the expenses incurred in equal proportions and shall pay such subscriptions and at such time as the President shall find necessary'. Since the President had powers 'to manage the Society, and with the

17

sanction of the majority of members, may do and order whatever he considers for its advantage', that may have been an expensive commitment. Since seven members were some wickets short of a team, visitors and occasional residents could be invited to play for the summer, but the exclusive nature of the club was ensured by a rule that permanent residents had to be vetted and have a written invitation from the President to play 'for the summer only'.

A second meeting on 28th June, decided that every Wednesday at 4.00 pm would be 'the time to meet and play in the field between Bessingby and the mill, but that if the weather do not permit meeting at that day, Friday be a meeting of course, if it then be favourable'. They clearly expected to attract people to watch, ordering benches for members at 8/- and sets of sticks to mark out the ground and restrain spectators from wandering on to the field of play.

It is probably significant that equipment had to be purchased from Allmut and Son, 186 Piccadilly, London rather than from a local company. Was there no firm in York capable of supplying 4 bats, 2 balls and a set of wickets and 'bales'? The equipment duly arrived at a cost of £2.14s.0d. and was itemised in the Club book. The two balls were recorded as 'Clout and Oaks' and 'Duke Pens', a reference to Dukes of Penshurst who had been making cricket balls since at least 1760. The four club bats were labelled 'Boynton-Baines and Oaks' and described as Crawle Maidstone (good), Clapshaw Farnham (good), Pawley Kennington (good, old?) and Eade Penshurst. Presumably these were different qualities of bats made by the two manufacturers.

The last entry of the Society was on 5th July 1820, when it was 'ordered that a piece of ground in the same field be prepared for playing in the future'. Nothing else is known of the Club. It is unlikely that it survived for very long and any fixtures that it did play went unrecorded.

It is only in the 1830's that local clubs begin to be mentioned. 'Hull at the present moment (1832) boasts of a most excellent cricket club, consisting of about 40 members, amongst whom are several crack players. Their ground is one of the meadows in the vicinity of Spring Bank, which is rolled and kept in order for the purpose'. The Hull Union C.C. played against the Officers and Privates of the 53rd Regiment in 1833. They attracted enough of the fashionable 'company' for the three match series to be accompanied by marquees and the regimental band. 'Nor must I forget the back stop

18

Rules of the Burlington
Cricket Society.
established June 1st. 1820

1st. That a society be formed called
the Burlington Cricket society
consisting of the gentlemen whose
names are annexed —

2. That on the application for the
admission of a new member, he
shall be balloted for, one black
ball to exclude & no ballot to
take place unless a majority of
the members are present. —

3. That a President be chosen
and Arthur Strickland Esqr
is appointed —

4. That the President shall trans-
=act the concerns of the society
& with the sanction of a majority
of the members may do & order
whatever he considers for its
advantage. —

5. That the Members shall be
answerable for the expenses
incurred in equal proportions —
while they such subscriptions
not such times as the President
shall require any to call for —

6. That a member may bring
with him or invite for the summer
any visitor or occasional resident
in the neighbourhood, but that
permanent residents shall be

Burlington Cricket Society Rules 1820.

of Mr. K. Maister, who, in spite of the swift bowling of his brother and receiving a very severe blow on his head, persevered at his post and only let his opponents run 11 byes in the two innings'.

A Hull Tyro Club visited Hyde Park in Sheffield to play the Sheffield Wednesday Club in 1835, but there is another long gap until 1841 before any further activity is reported. 'The steady upward progress from 1824'[3] that has been noted nationally only comes about from 1841 locally. From that date there is a flurry of activity and a mushrooming of clubs both in Hull and the Riding. The Albion Club played on Anlaby Road. The Amateur Club started the 1842 season with regular practices and reported an increased membership. Hull Kingston was playing in the same year. The Beverley Law Club played a 'superior' Hovingham side on the Westwood and Charles Cartman and Leonard Hobson played a single wicket match for five sovereigns on the West Green at Pocklington.

Cricket was established in the local schools at least by 1839 when St. Peter's played the Collegiate School on the Knavesmire. Beverley Grammar School, playing on the Westwood, had fixtures against Kingston College and Pocklington Grammar School in 1849. The latter played 'on the new Pocklington ground'. The teams seem to have been a mixture of senior boys and staff. Many of the boys would be boarders from the East Riding, which would encourage the formation of clubs in their own home district once they had left school.

The local perception of all this activity was quite clearly that this was a revival of interest in a game that had been in decline. 'We are glad to perceive that the game of cricket, which has hitherto been principally confined to the Northern and Midland counties, is becoming more popular further north'. (1843) Across the river, Barton formed a side in 1844, 'upwards of 12 years since a cricket club existed in the town'. The editor could write in the same year that 'it gives us great pleasure to note the spread of cricket in Yorkshire and the north of England'.

In view of these comments, it is difficult to argue against the conclusion that not very much cricket was being played locally in the 1830's and that the game only regained popularity and achieved a secure footing in the area after 1841. After that date there is the 'steady upward progress' of the national scene. The local dearth is all the more annoying because it was during this period that under-arm bowling gave way to round-arm. At the moment there is just not sufficient evidence to explain either the decline or the revival in interest.

Whatever the reasons, cricket went from strength to strength in Hull, with the Hull Kingston Club, playing 'on the ground behind Mr. Beecroft's on the Anlaby Road', emerging as the premier side in the city. They quickly established an ambitious fixture list that took them into Lincolnshire to play Gainsborough as well as into the Riding. All the leading Hull clubs played against the regiments garrisoned at the Citadel, which like all army bases, had its own cricket ground. Kingston came under fire when they lost to the 40th Foot in 1847. 'The garrison players are neither batsmen nor bowlers, but still they proved themselves capable of beating the cracks, who previous to the commencement of the game, would have had plenty of supporters at odds. The Hull club certainly have two or three clever players, but unless they occasionally receive the aid of others, defeat is certain'. When they played the Albion Club, a junior side, 'four of the principal players of Kingston (were) barred', a common way of matching two unequal sides.

The St. George's Club was not far behind in stature. They played in 'a cricket shirt, white flannel with red cross on left arm, white trousers and a cricket hat bound in red', but it was the patrician Hull Athenaeum Club which was responsible for the most significant advance of cricket in the area. They were formed in 1848 and like the Kingston Club played in Anlaby Road, indeed it is probable, but not certain, that they shared the ground behind the Brown Cow Inn, between Ocean Place and Great Thornton Street, with the Kingston side. They were soon considered to be a team 'likely to attain national celebrity'. They certainly had the economic confidence and sufficient self-belief to arrange 'a very adventurous undertaking on the part of a club so recently formed', a three-day game against the All-England Eleven for July 1849.

William Clarke's All-England Eleven was formed in 1846 as a body of touring professionals who were prepared to play against local opposition in any part of the country. They were, first and foremost, a business, aiming to make money for the top professionals who were in Clarke's company, but because they were the leading cricketers of the time, they often included the most talented amateurs in their ranks. They were sometimes criticised by contemporaries for their 'aim after lucre'[4] but even their critics

21

conceded that they did much to spread enthusiasm for the game around the regions and raise the standards of locals clubs.

Clarke brought the equivalent of a Test side to Hull. It included three all-time greats, Fuller Pilch, Felix and Alfred Mynn. Pilch, a professional throughout his career, dominated the era in which he played, standing 'head and shoulders above his contemporaries'. He was the first batsman to combine front and back-foot play and was, in the opinion of one historian of the game, 'of the stature relatively, of W. G. Grace, and his performances compare strictly with Grace's statistically'.[5] Alfred Mynn, like Felix an amateur, stood over 6′ and weighed 18 stones, 'being as fine a specimen of an Englishman in appearance as could be desired' in the opinion of the *Hull Advertiser*. He was genuinely very fast and unlike many round-arm bowlers of the time, very accurate. He was a powerful and effective batsman, but probably not as good as Felix, the third all-rounder in the trio. Felix, (Nicholas Wanostrocht), had taught himself to play Mynn's fast bowling by practising against a bowling machine, the catapulta, which he had developed from a Roman model. If these three were not formidable enough opposition, number three in the All-England Eleven was George Parr of Nottinghamshire, 'the England Pet' who captained the first English touring side of 1859, which toured Canada and the United States. William Clarke was an interesting character himself, in that he reverted to under-arm bowling and was said to be as fast as any round-arm bowler of the time.

Against this formidable side was assembled 22 of Hull and District. 'About half are from the district and that number again divided between Yorkshire and Lincolnshire'. Five players can be identified as playing for the Hull Athenaeum or Kingston Clubs, two are obviously local army officers and R. Bickers played for Beverley. It is possible that Potts and Lead were two professionals, but if so, it is surprising that they did not bowl.

One of the reasons why the match was considered 'a very adventurous undertaking' was the financial risk involved. A large gate would need to be attracted over the three days to cover Clarke's fees and the expenses of staging such a fixture. The Committee of Management secured the patronage and, in effect, sponsorship from various local worthies such as the Sheriff and the two local M.P.'s. The ground was ideally situated close to Hull's original railway station, which allowed spectators who had travelled on the cheap

22

fares negotiated with the railway companies to move easily from the station into the ground. Nevertheless the entrance fee of 1/- a day caused surprise, especially when one of the professionals let it be known that the normal admission at their games was about half that. There was some concern also about the suitability of the ground, which 'though one of the largest fields in the neighbourhood is too small for the purposes of such a match'. The pitch 'between and near the wickets has been prepared and is as even as could be desired' but nothing much could be done about the outfield, 'the greatest portion of which is in ridges. Several of the All-England gentlemen expressed considerable distaste' at the prospect of fielding on it.

Nevertheless the committee's arrangements worked well. The six acre ground was screened by new canvas to a height of several feet, which was easier to achieve in 19th Century Hull of course, than in many places. Three sides were lined with tents and pavilions for refreshments etc., whilst the largest tent, normally to be found housing the exhibitions at the Botanic Gardens, was set aside for the ladies. Lillywhite's portable press occupied a small tent, as it did at all Clarke's matches, printing score-cards at the fall of each wicket.

One factor that could not be controlled was the weather, which was showery, dull and overcast. The start was delayed and the first day's attendance was less than a thousand. There was not much betting on the match as most people felt that the locals had been over optimistic in challenging All-England. The score-card is given in the Appendix.

All-England batted through until the late afternoon of the second day against the bowling of Lambert, Bickers, Parker and a slow bowler, Taylor. 28 wides probably tell their own story, but Parker would long remember the match in which he captured the wickets of Pilch, Mynn and Felix in one innings! Chatterton scored very quickly, 'now and then giving a boother', which was presumably hitting the ball into or over one of the tents. Felix 'struck a ball very hard up in the air; Mr. Fisher in attempting to catch it, let it pass through his hands on to his face, which caused him to retire'. The professionals had little difficulty bowling out the 22 twice on the Saturday to win by an innings and 82 runs. 'The fears entertained of Hull having prematurely matched themselves with All-England were too well founded. The long training, incessant practice and renowned skill of the latter decided the match'.

Whatever the result, the match had been significant. There was never again to be any lack of popularity for the game in the area. The professionals had been brought to Hull because there was enough interest in the area already to justify the invitation. They did not cause the subsequent expansion of the game locally, but no doubt they contributed to it. What is beyond all doubt is that over the next twenty years, clubs were formed in many areas of the East Riding where none had existed before.

Sources:

[1]   R. Bowen. *Cricket: A History of its Growth and Development throughout the World* 1970. Pages 79-80.

[2]   An unpublished document in the possession of the late Mr. J. Wood, Bridlington C.C.

[3]   Bowen p. 80.

[4]   Box p. 251.

[5]   Bowen p. 96.

CRICKET AND THE BOOKIES

If the Beverley Club was combining the visit to Doncaster with a trip to the St. Leger in 1825, it was merely continuing a long tradition which linked cricket to the bookmakers. It is a commonplace that early cricket matches were played for high stakes under the patronage of the nobility. Indeed it seems likely that the first collections of batting statistics were as much in the interests of studying recent form as for any other purpose. It was also one reason why scorers changed from cutting notches on sticks to recording performances with pen and paper. An accurate record was needed to settle bets. In the same way early score-cards often don't name the bowler when the dismissal was lbw, stumped, sometimes even caught, because the bowler was not seen as responsible for the dismissal and it could not be counted in any bet on his performance. Hit wicket was a particularly difficult area. As declarations were not allowed, batsmen sometimes deliberately broke their wicket to bring an innings to a close. Scoring with pen and paper did not always solve the problems. When ten men of Escrick played ten men of Fulford in 1833, 'the Escrick players were declared the winners by 1 notch and 4 wickets to go down; but owing to a dispute between the bookkeepers, which could not be decided, both contending that they were right and their differences only being 1 notch, the stakes were withdrawn'.

Betting remained a constant feature of the game well into the Victorian period and at every level, including those far removed from the influence of the nobility. In 1861 an evening match between Lund and Driffield Victoria produced a tie on the first innings. Amid great excitement, before the start of the second innings, 'a good many bets were made on the game, evens being freely offered and taken by the friends of both clubs'. They then adjourned to the Black Swan for dinner and having spent 'an agreeable and merry day, left for their homes about 10.00 in the evening'. The pub is the other constant in cricket, usually in close proximity to the ground and sometimes providing the ground.

The notion of 'a match' often implied playing for a stake. When

25

the Kirkbymoorside Club lost heavily to Malton in August 1833, they immediately challenged their opponents to a return match at 50 guineas a side. When more fashionable clubs met at a venue that attracted 'the company' in large numbers, then the betting became as important as the game itself. The York Club played the Harewood Club on the Knavesmire in 1833. The betting began with the odds at 6 to 4 against York, hardened to 4 to 1 after the first innings, but swung to 2 to 1 on after Harewood lost five cheap wickets in the second innings. It was not just the spectators who bet on the changing fortunes of the game. 'Letby took 2 to 1 that he scored 50, which number he exactly obtained'. It all proved too exciting for some. 'The game terminated in a tie, in consequence of one of the last in, throwing up his bat whilst the ball was on the ground and crying out 'we've won' when the fact was that they had only got the same number of notches as the Yorkers had. After some little altercation, each agreed to draw their stakes'. 'A little altercation' may have been an understatement!

There was always the danger that the betting could dominate proceedings. Letby might not have got out when he did, if he had not just won his bet. The other suspicion was that matches would be 'sold', but if that was ever the case locally, no local newspaper editor seems to have been willing to risk the courts by voicing his suspicions. Incidentally, Richard Letby was the landlord of the Cricketers Arms in York for 24 years. He had a formidable throw and once lost a wager despite throwing a ball 105 yards. In the 1830's he clearly made a very good living by backing himself to win cricket matches either single handedly or with a partner. As his reputation grew, he had to look further afield for opponents, who were drawn from all over the north of England. When he finished playing he umpired York's matches for many years.

It was this form of cricket, that pitched one man in direct conflict with another, that produced the most sporting interest. The single wicket match is a version of the game that has disappeared, at least in its 18th and 19th Century form. In 1866 after a match between Hull and Malton, George Freeman was challenged by Mr. H. Terry of Hull, who had scored 29 out of a Hull total of 34. Both men were well-known throughout the area and there was considerable speculation about the result. Freeman, who was from Borough-bridge, played for both the Malton Club, which was probably the strongest local side in the 1860's and for the United All-England

Eleven. Freeman was the best fast bowler of his time and 'the first of Yorkshire's indisputably great bowlers'.[1] A contemporary in the Yorkshire side, Ephraim Lockwood, said that 'he used to make the ball come back six inches, whipping like lightning from the pitch. It was done with a remarkable whip of the wrist'. He had made his Yorkshire debut in 1865 taking 51 wickets at an average of 7.4 runs. At the time of the challenge, he formed a formidable opening attack for Yorkshire with Tom Emmett, the pair bowling throughout the match on no fewer than six occasions.[2] Freeman took 209 wickets in 32 matches for Yorkshire and must have been a fearsome prospect for local batsmen when he played against them for Malton. W. G. Grace stated that being hit on the leg by Freeman was like 'being cut by a knife'.

He matched himself for £50 against Terry, who put up £25. The terms of the match allowed each man to nominate his own fielder and an umpire. Freeman had the choice of ground which was to be declared a month before the date fixed for the game. He chose to play on the Old Ground at York, picked Dewse of York as his fielder and Lightowler of Malton as his umpire. Lee, a professional from Leeds was the other umpire and Ullathorne did the fielding for Terry. Freeman was the clear favourite at 3 to 1 on, but both men attracted considerable support throughout the Riding. It was claimed that £1000 was staked on the issue in Beverley alone, a considerable sum of money for 1866. The match was won by Freeman who scored 24 and 5 in his two innings, against Terry's scores of 1 and 0.

There is a fuller description of a second match played in 1866 at Beverley, which is worth looking at in detail because it reveals more of the nature of the game. It could be played with up to six men in each team, but its purest form was between two individuals such as Freeman and Terry. A run was 'there and back' and the batsman had to knock the bail off the two (not three) stumps at the bowler's end. The batsman was not allowed to leave his crease to come down the wicket to the bowling and scoring was restricted to certain areas. All scoring had to be in front of the wicket and 'bounds shall be placed 22 yds. each, in a line from the off and leg stumps'.[3]

The tactics of the game were presumably for the bowler to field the straight drives and to bowl at either the leg stump or the off stump, with the single fielder guarding the square hit on whichever side the bowler was concentrating his attack. One wonders what success a modern limited overs specialist would have in such a situation, backing away to leg in order to create room to hit a leg stump ball through an empty off side. Given the wickets of 1866 the contest may have favoured the bowler.

The fielder did not have to run the batsman out in order to prevent a run being scored. Once the return throw had broken any of the 'bounds', the ball was dead and if the batsman had not completed his 'double run' no score was counted.

> 'If the striker in running have knocked off the bail upon the opposite wicket and return home before the ball have struck down his wicket, or cross the play, or been between the bounds and his own wicket, it is to be considered a run'.[4]

Given accurate bowling directed at one stump and an athletic fielder with a fast throw, it becomes understandable that scoring was often found difficult. It is also possible to see how such a contest could attract a great deal of interest, particularly if the batsman was prepared to take on the fielder.

The match at Beverley was for a £60 stake between two amateurs, G. Barker of Sessay near Thirsk and Thomas Green of the Turf Inn, Beverley. Sessay, one of the strongest North Riding sides in the 1860's, frequently played in Hull against Hull Kingston and Hull Mechanics. Green, who appears in several Hull and Beverley score-cards, was to put up £40 of the stake. As before both men nominated an umpire and their single fieldsman. The fielder was clearly a crucial choice and Green picked the same man that Terry had chosen in the earlier match, Charlie Ullathorne of Hull, a Yorkshire county player, who proved 'an excellent choice, winning the applause of the spectators for his excellent fielding and splendid throws'. Barker retained Carver of York, 'a well-known cricketer in the North Riding' as his fielder and North of Thirsk as the umpire.

Green won the toss to choose the ground and resisting pressure to play the match at York, brought it to his home ground on the Westwood. Barker started as the 2 to 1 favourite and was priced at 6 to 4 when Green won the toss and put him into bat. Barker was caught and bowled off the eighth delivery for 0. The betting was at evens when Green went into bat against 'some masterly bowling. Playing with remarkable caution' he survived 25 balls without scoring, before losing his leg stump.

In the second innings, Barker drove his 6th, 8th and 11th balls for one. The 15th 'was hit straight beautifully, but only for one'. He scored off the 18th but was bowled leg stump off the 21st for 6. 'At this stage odds were freely laid on Barker. Green faced some superior bowling, the back balls being played well'. He had scored 2 to the off and 1 for a straight drive, when the field was changed from the on to the off side. He added two singles off the 26th and 42nd balls to take his score to 5. At this stage the odds swung to 2 to 1 on Green, 'but he found the bowling most difficult to get off' and was bowled by a shooter off the 18th to lose by one run. There was general agreement that Barker's bowling was superior to any seen on the Westwood for several years.

Such matches between the leading players of the area attracted a lot of interest and not just from the betting fraternity. There was a spate of single wicket games in Hull after these two matches, played by ordinary club players. This form of cricket remained popular and a game was often improvised when a normal match ended quickly. No doubt they were often played for a wager and settled in the pub at the end of play. The last single wicket match to be noted in the area was in 1899 when Waites of Lund played against Simpson of Middleton.

Sources:
[1] Hodgson. *The Official History of Yorkshire County Cricket Club*. The Crowood Press 1989, p. 18.

[2] Ibid p. 309.

[3] Box p. 375.

[4] John Nyren. *The Young Cricketer's Tutor 1833*. Edited by C. C. Clarke 1974, p. 48.

BEVERLEY v DRIFFIELD 1863

It is possible to get something of the flavour of Victorian cricket by looking at two matches played between Beverley and Driffield in 1863. Despite the excellent relationship between the two clubs, there is always an extra edge to these games, which since the introduction of league cricket in the 20th Century, have usually been played on the bank holidays. It is not surprising to see this rivalry going back into the 19th Century.

The first game in 1863 was played at Beverley before 'a great number of people on the ground'. As was normal the game was played over two innings commencing at 11.00, the equivalent of 12.00 in today's British Summer Time. The length of the game presented a problem in the 1860's. The playing conditions always favoured the bowlers since there is little to suggest that wickets were prepared in any meaningful way. As a consequence the scores were low. 50 to 60 runs seems to have been a respectable total for an innings. A single innings match was therefore always likely to be over very quickly. On the other hand, a two innings game was not often completed before stumps were drawn, a time that was often dictated by the local railway timetable and the need of the visiting side to catch their train home. The practice in unfinished games was not to call them a draw, but to judge them on the basis of the 1st innings. This could produce some strange anomalies to modern eyes. In a game between Driffield and Bridlington in 1865, Driffield scored 48 and 35 for 8, whilst Bridlington scored 30 and 104. Driffield was judged to have won the match on the basis of the 1st innings. This method of deciding a result must have had some interesting tactical implications.

A similar result occurred in the first Beverley-Driffield game in the 1863 season.

The score-card is unremarkable, though it is worth pointing out that a game that produced only three run outs is well below the average. It is not uncommon to see three in a single innings, perhaps as a consequence of the absence of boundaries, which meant that all hits had to be run. Hit wicket was also a much more common form of dismissal than in the modern game.

30

BEVERLEY v DRIFFIELD
Played at Beverley, Wednesday 8th July 1863
Wickets pitched at 11.00 a.m.

DRIFFIELD:	1st Innings			2nd Innings	
Rev. C. Day	c Scarboro'	b Bickers	2	hit wkt b Hind	25
Kirkby		b Hind	3	not out	2
Matthews	c and	b Hind	0	b Bickers	0
A. Botterill	not out		18	b Whatham	10
Cattle	c Scarboro'	b Hind	0	b Hind	4
Railton		b Bickers	0	b Hind	1
Teal	run out		12	run out	0
Holtby		b Hind	1	b Hind	0
Hewson	c Sumner	b Hind	6	b Hind	7
Shepherd		b Bickers	5	c Hepworth b Hind	5
Extras 4b			4	Extras 8b 1w	9
			52		65

BEVERLEY:	1st Innings			2nd Innings	
Grant		b Railton	2	c Shepherd b Railton	4
Whattam	c Day	b Railton	2		
Scarborough		b Railton	0		
Stephenson	c Day	b Railton	0		
Hind	lbw	b Railton	7	b Day	4
Parnell		b Day	0	not out	14
Green	lbw	b Railton	11	c Cattle b Day	0
Bickers	run out		11	not out	18
Hepworth		b Railton	2		
Musgrave		b Day	6		
Sumner	not out		1		
Extras 3b 3 1b			6	Extras 4b 3 1b	7
			48		47

Driffield won on the basis of the 1st Innings

Driffield's Captain, Christopher Day, 'of whom great things were anticipated' was 'cleverly caught at short slip' in the first innings and in the second innings was 'cleverly got by tactics which are worth noticing. Hind gave Mr. Day a ball nearly up to the popping crease,

31

which he drove away; directly after however Hind had his revenge, for he gave him another straight one, but short pitched. The Reverend Gentleman in his hurry to play back, was driven on to his own wicket'. The excellent longstopping of Sumner was picked out. Beverley fell victim 'principally to Railton who (in the opinion of the *Beverley Guardian*) bowled in thorough windmill fashion and who ought to have been no-balled every ball'. In the second innings, Beverley needing 70 to win before stumps at 7.00 pm decided 'to hit at all hazards', but ended at 47 for 3.

The Driffield victory clearly stung Beverley into taking the return match very seriously. The Driffield Secretary wrote to his opposite number offering Friday 16th August for the fixture, but was told that Beverley could not play on that day. Most games seem to have been arranged on this basis at a few days notice. Fixture lists were unusual. In this instance the *Driffield Times* clearly suspected a degree of gamesmanship.

Having refused the Friday, 'the Beverlonians apparently were very active in the meantime, getting up their best eleven, which having been completed, they sent word on the Saturday that they wished to play the return match on the Monday. This of course took the Driffield Secretary by surprise and gave no time for communicating with members residing at a distance, who, unfortunately, are the bowling strength of the club'.

The game began at 11.00, 'it could not be called a match inasmuch as the sides were far from equal', with Driffield making heavy weather of the bowling of Whattam, who 'showed a good deal of science', and of Hind, the Beverley professional. Like many round-arm bowlers of this period, he pushed the law to its limit by delivering the ball at, or just above shoulder height. If the umpire was not to be decapitated by a right arm over the wicket round-arm bowler, he would have to stand well back. Indeed, given the need to watch the back foot for no-balls at the same time as judging the height of the bowling arm at the shoulder, the umpire could not have stood close to the wicket. Whatever the umpires thought, the Driffield crowd objected to Hind's bowling. Ironically in view of the *Beverley Guardian*'s comments on the bowling of Railton in the first match, the *Driffield Times* wrote that 'many questions were asked by the spectators as to whether Hind's style was legitimate, as he invariably delivered the ball above the shoulder: for ourselves we are pretty sure that it would not be allowed amongst professionals as it would be called nothing else but pelting'.

These comments are particularly interesting in that over-arm bowling became legal the following year, in June 1864. In one sense this marks a watershed in the game, but the change seems to have had little effect locally and was not remarked upon. It is probable that most bowlers continued much as before, with the arm at or about shoulder height. There is no more reason to suppose that bowlers suddenly adopted a vertical arm than to suppose that round-arm bowling had immediately replaced all under-arm bowling in local matches thirty years before.

The teams took an early lunch when rain forced them off, but in the afternoon Beverley bowled out Driffield for 55 and scored 80 in their own first innings, though their tactics were not appreciated. 'There was not a single good hit from the beginning to the end of the innings', instead they were content to 'steal notches'. What was worse, 'a certain "Greenhorn" observed that he thought he could have stopped in all day'. Whattam and Hyde whipped out the Driffield 2nd innings, leaving the visitors needing only 8 for victory.

The home side may have been short of their best bowlers, but Hewson had a splendid match, taking nine wickets, 'whilst Mr. Matthews was wonderfully active at the stumps'.

It is perhaps worth pointing out that whilst 'runs' continued to be called 'notches' it must have been a long time before 1863 that a scorer had used anything other than a pen and paper to record the score. The score-card also shows the Beverley professional's (Hind's) contribution, 9 wickets and 22*, the highest score of the match, this despite receiving 'a severe blow to the body' forcing him to retire for a short time.

This was not the only occasion when it was felt in Driffield that Beverley's eagerness to win overstepped the mark. A junior club in the town, Driffield Victoria, played Beverley Mechanics and lost. When the return game was played on Beverley Westwood 'it was intended to be a return match between the above clubs, but the Beverlonians after their bombastical and exaggerated account of their triumphs over the Victoria in their last contest could not afford a defeat and so to ensure a second victory, the best cricketers in Beverley were pressed into the contest and the small fry withdrawn to make room for them. Yet this immense advantage obtained by such unfair means failed to secure them the coveted victory'.

DRIFFIELD v BEVERLEY
Played at Shady Lane, Driffield, Monday 12th July 1863
Wickets pitched at 11.00 a.m.

DRIFFIELD:

	1st Innings			2nd Innings	
Teal		b Hind	0	c Hind b Whattam	3
Kirkby	c Green	b Whattam	0	b Whattam	1
Cattle	c Compton	b Hind	0	run out	2
Hewson		b Whattam	9	c Whattam b Hind	6
Matthews		b Hind	13	not out	12
Duggleby		b Whattam	4	b Whattam	0
H. Botterill	not out		6	b Hind	0
Shepherd		b Whattam	2	c Compton b Hind	0
Burton		b Whattam	2	c Compton b Whattam	0
Cumming		b Hind	1	c and b Hind	7
Holtby	run out		6	b Hind	0
Extras			12	Extras	1
			55		32

BEVERLEY:

	1st Innings			2nd Innings	
Green		b Hewson	15		
Hepworth	c Teal	b Hewson	0	not out	5
Whattam	st Matthews	b Teal	5		
Grant		b Hewson	2		
Hind	not out		22		
Boyes		b Hewson	3		
Sumner		b Hewson	9		
Compton	c Shepherd	b Hewson	0	b Hewson	2
Padget	run out		9		
Farrah	c Teal	b Hewson	2		
Chalmes	run out		1	lbw b Hewson	0
Extras			12	Extras	2
			80	2 for	9

Beverley won by 8 wickets

No doubt such grievances grew in the telling and helped to develop the rivalry between the two towns in subsequent seasons.

34

STANDARDS AND PERFORMANCES 1850-1870

When John Nyren wrote *The Young Cricketer's Tutor* in 1833, he included a section on the standard field placings and the qualities that were needed to fill each position. A flavour of the work may be had from the description of Long Field Straight On 'who should stand at some distance out from the bowler's wicket to save the two runs. When the bowling can be depended on, and the hitting is not severe, he may be brought into save the one run. At Long Field to the Hip, the fieldsman must stand out to save two runs opposite the popping crease. Every person who takes the long field should be able to throw well, to run well and he should begin to run before the ball is struck: this, in the language of cricket, is called getting the start of the ball'.[1]

The names used by Nyren and the basic field set seem to have lasted in local cricket into the 1860's. The only variation noted is a reference to long leg in 1864, but there are very few references to fielding positions in the reports on matches. The exceptions are longstop and point, which were regarded as the key positions. The fielder at longstop, usually a specialist who fielded there at both ends, is often mentioned by name and singled out for praise. It was seen as being a difficult and even a dangerous place to field. The only description of a field setting is contained in a report of an All-England match in 1867 when the professionals, who were in danger of losing to Hull, successfully pressurised the last few batsmen by crowding the bat. Tactics rarely get a mention, though Beverley was criticised by the *Driffield Times* for 'resorting to the somewhat questionable expedient of concentrating all their skill on one batsman by frequently changing the field'. By 1871, short legs, mid-wicket, long on and mid-off are being mentioned and just occasionally a field setting creeps into the description of an important match.

The out-fields could not have been easy to field on. The disdain of the All-England professionals when they were asked to play on the Westwood and on the ridge and furrow of Hull's ground was understandable. A start was made at levelling out that ground in 1856 but it was a long time before other clubs paid very much attention to their out-fields. At Brandesburton for example, the number of byes in one match, 20 out of a total of 50 runs, 'must be accounted for owing to the roughness of the ground behind the wickets'.

One factor in raising the standard of the club cricketers was the tuition of the professional. There are many glowing tributes to the improvements that they brought about, particularly by bowling to the members in the nets, which was one of their prime responsibilities. It may have been much more difficult for the pro. to influence the fielding, though he may have helped to develop a sense of tactics and cricketing awareness. 'We can hardly say too much of the improvement which Mr. Crossland has effected in the (Hull) Town Club and in his general management of the field'. The management of the field is a term that was often used to describe the captain's duties and a popular and respected pro. like Crossland, may well have been in tactical control on the field, but as a paid servant of a gentleman's club he would have had to bite his tongue at any fielding lapses.

'One gentleman in particular was the frequent object of remark, for although he let several balls slip, as it were, through him and seemed to field without freedom of action, yet under no consideration could he be prevailed upon to take off his waistcoat and try to do better. It was whispered it was thought it set off his figure, but it is really a matter of regret, if such was the case, that vanity should give place to efficiency'.

In the end it may be that simply playing alongside several professionals raised the standard of the amateurs. After all, an amateur playing in the Hull v Malton match of 1866 was in the company of Dewse, Freeman, Crossland, Job Greenwood and Ullathorne. The last named in particular, established a reputation as a brilliant fielder. 'The ball appeared to be dropping half-way to the boundary, but Ullathorne dashed towards it with full speed, just reached it and rolled over with it clasped in his hands'. In a match against Dewsbury, 'Perkins was splendidly thrown out at a distance of over 50 yards by Ullathorne, who stopped a hard hit to deep mid-on and returned the ball so quickly that the batsman was out before he reached mid-wicket'. He was Terry's choice of fielder in his single wicket match against Freeman, who chose Dewse. Hull probably set the standards, the other clubs perhaps, followed more slowly. It is not difficult to find examples which suggest that the

36

2

4

3

1
⌴

5

11

6

7

9

8

10

1. wicket—keeper.
2. long—stop.
3. short slip.
4. long slip.
5. the point of the bat.
6. long field to cover the middle wicket and point.
7. the middle wicket.
8. long—field straight off.
9. bowler.
10. long—field straight on.
11. long—field to the hip.

The fielding positions given by Nyren.

fielding sometimes left much to be desired. 'Beverley exhibited an apathy in the field which told much in favour of their opponents. It has been hinted too that success in future would be more likely to ensue if the members displayed greater unity in the field and assisted the captain in performing his functions'. Nevertheless the tone of reports by 1870 suggest that the fielding in many clubs had improved and was being taken seriously.

There is no doubt that some of the clubs had specialist wicket-keepers. Morton, who played for the Beverley District Eleven, Wise of Malton and Twiss, who was playing with Hull in 1865, were clearly specialists, but in the majority of clubs the practice seems to have been for the bowler to move behind the stumps when he had finished his own over. Perhaps this helps to explain why a good longstop was so essential. There can be no other explanation for so many score-cards of the period, which show bowlers both taking wickets and stumping batsmen in the same innings. Matthews of Driffield, who was 'wonderfully active at the stumps' against Beverley in 1863, was one of the club's main bowlers. Heseltine, who was Londesborough Park's professional in 1862, took 7 wickets and a stumping in one innings. Teal and Dunn, two regular bowlers, both claimed a stumping for Driffield in the same innings against Scarborough in 1870. Pinkney of Filey had the rare distinction of being stumped in both innings by two different wicket-keepers. Even at the more sophisticated clubs, Crossland stumped a Leeds batsman off his fellow professional, Greenwood, and claimed another stumping against Gainsborough in an innings in which he also bowled. A Hull v Malton score-card of 1871 shows a dismissal 'st Dewse b Iddison'. It may be significant that when Morton was injured keeping wicket against the All-England Eleven, it was Arnold, one of the professional bowlers, who took over behind the stumps. There seems to have been a change towards 1870, perhaps influenced by the more frequent engagement of professional bowlers, who may have encouraged specialist wicket-keeping as much from self-interest as for any other reason.

Bowling throughout the period to 1870 (and beyond) was a mixture of round-arm and under-arm. Such descriptions as 'Piercey (round) and Teal (under-hand) opened the bowling', are common and evoke no surprise. 'Mr. Truswell (slow, under-hand) ' bowled for All-England in 1869 and Lyons of Bridlington was bowling 'daisy-cutters' in 1873. It means that all the score-cards from this period reflect the two kinds of bowling, though there is no doubt that round-arm was much the more common.

Even the most cursory glance at these score-cards reveals the way the ball dominated the bat. Bowen in his book[2] has an interesting section on the way in which the introduction of round-arm bowling restricted scoring. He shows that the main batting records in the first class game, that were set in the under-arm age, remained as records until well into the round-arm period. For example, the highest individual score, 278, was not beaten until 1865. Even more significantly, he found that in 1828, for every 100 matches there were 45 fifties, a figure that was not beaten until 1858.

The domination of ball over bat is much more marked in the East Riding. Between 1850 and 1869, at every level of cricket, ranging from All-England matches, Club first and second elevens to village sides, there are only 29 scores of fifty or more that have been noted. Two of the 29 went on to make centuries, 101 by Stainsby of Hull against Lincoln in 1856 and 108 by Burton of Driffield in a bizarre game to be discussed in a later chapter. Crossland had three of the fifties, including an heroic 98 out of 140 against Newark. The general level of expectation may be seen from one report in 1861 in which 'two or three of the players succeeded in making large scores' which proved to be 20, 15 and 14. When Bickers of Beverley was 'thrown out by Cook for 21' at Hornsea, he 'was chaired and carried shoulder height to the tents amidst the cheers of the spectators',

An analysis of seventeen score-cards between 1860 and 1866, chosen to include fourteen of the more prominent club sides in the area, is revealing.[3] Almost all the games involved professionals, sometimes up to three a side. The average team score for the 43 completed innings was 59 runs. There were only seven team scores of over 100 and the highest individual score was 63. That these scores are not unusual may be seen from the batting averages. The earliest example to be found locally is in 1865 when figures were given for Driffield in a very abbreviated form. The top three batsmen were:

J. Hopper   3 matches average 13
F. Shepherd   5 matches average 13
R. Teal   7 matches average 11

The only other averages published in this period are those of Bridlington for 1866, Beverley in 1868 and 1870 and Hull for 1870:

	Inns	Runs	H.S.	Most in a match	N.O.	Ave.
A. Wood	6	72	24	24	2	12.0
W. Lee	7	83	22*	28	4	11.6
J. Burman (pro)	12	87	34	34	1	7.3
L. Wallgate	6	31	18	24	0	5.1
C. Ullathorne	9	45	9	14	0	5.0

(The average was evidently based on the number of innings and included the not outs)[4].

It may not be obvious from the Hull averages, including as they do a professional and two Yorkshire County players, but there was a marked improvement in 1870 when 8 scores of fifty are recorded, including 169 by the Cambridge batsman, J. Smith, against Leeds. He does not appear in the averages, presumably because he only played the one game. From 1871 onwards there is a distinct rise in the totals achieved by Hull and their opponents. Team scores of 200 or more are quite common and in 1875 Lt. Hodder hit 203* for Hull, 'the highest score on the ground'. Such a marked change must reflect a significant improvement in the wickets. It was about this time that Hull began to engage two professionals each season, one of whom seems to have been regarded primarily as the groundsman and net bowler. It is also possible to detect in the reports on Hull's matches, a definite sense of pride in the quality of the wickets provided and an increasingly critical view of other club's wickets, that did not come up to the same standard.

The local clubs that had fixtures at Argyle St. would no doubt be impressed by playing on better surfaces and do their best to improve their own wickets. There are signs that batting standards were slowly improving. In 1870 'a new match bat, offered by the (Beverley) Club for any member who could succeed in making 50 runs in one innings in any of the club matches .... has been offered for two years past and is now won for the first time'.

It is tempting to attribute the low scoring before 1870 solely to poor wickets. Almost every 19th Century speech extollng the virtues of cricket, runs through the clichés that it is a manly game, character building, a sport fit for true Englishmen etc., in much the same terms as were used about boxing. Behind the phrases, is the unspoken assumption that it was part of the game to stand up and take a degree of punishment. The youngsters of the Driffield Albert Club in 1864 may have had some justification when 'it was very plain they all played in fear'. At Market Weighton 'the balls bumped and fluked considerably'. Mr. Musgrave took 'a severe blow on his cheek which caused him to retire'. There can be little doubt that before 1870 wickets were untrustworthy and remained so for some time after in the case of the smaller clubs.

Only two East Riding score-cards exist from the under-arm period, which does not give enough local material to compare with the 1860's, but it is possible that one other reason for the low scoring is that it may have been difficult to score from round-arm bowling. Nyren's field has a packed off-side. If a round-arm bowler, bowled across a batsman to a 7-2 field, he may have been very hard to get away. Left-handed round-arm, like the Beverley pro. Kenyon, would present a very different line of attack and reports suggest that local batsmen found him very difficult to handle. On the other hand in the seventeen matches considered earlier, 51.4% of the dismissals were bowled, which does not suggest that bowlers were bowling wide of the off-stump. 30.9% were caught. The absence of boundaries may also have contibuted to low scores, as all scoring shots had to be run. It may also help to explain why an incredible 11% of the dismissals were run outs. The other statistics are 3.8% L.B.W., 2% stumped and 0.9% hit wicket. In the end, true over-arm bowling may have been easier to score from because it opened up both sides of the wicket. That factor, together with professional coaching and greater attention to wickets through the use of marl, loam and a heavy roller, may well help to explain why, at all levels of local club cricket, the balance tilted in favour of the batsmen in the 1880's.

Even in the 1860's there were one or two local batsmen who did succeed in making an impression. The Rev. Christopher Day, who played for Driffield, Hull, the village side Langtoft and many another side, was a considerable all-rounder. His 'sharp' and 'swift bowling' took many wickets, but his 47 and 56 in one match against Brandesburton was very exceptional for the period and a 55* against Beverley was described as 'a brilliant display of hitting and defence'. Terry and Stainsby of Hull, Green of Beverley, Day and another clergyman, the Rev. E. B. Kay, seem to have been among the very few local amateurs who could score consistently.

The employment of club professionals became widespread in the 1860's. Some clubs used three or four at a time for important games.

Beverley had a close connection with Richard Daft, a leading player with the All-England side and Nottinghamshire, who knew the Beverley ground from the days that he played in the area before his professional career. He was approached by the club to recommend a professional to them in 1863, but he pointed out that by that time, April, all the leading players had contracts. He suggested W. Hind, 'middle-aged, but active, a nice medium paced bowler', who had in an emergency once played for the All-England Eleven, which was the equivalent of test status. Beverley engaged him for ten weeks and were sufficiently pleased to extend his contract for a further six. Driffield first employed a professional, T. Brown in 1867 and felt that 'the club doing remarkably well is attributable mainly to the tuition and assiduity of Brown', but they did not re-engage him for 1868 and did without a professional for several years.

Andrew Crossland was a regular member of the All-England Eleven and the Yorkshire side in the 1850's. He settled in Hull when his first-class career was over and earned a living as a pro. with most of the Hull clubs, as well as many of those in the Riding when they felt the need to strengthen their sides for a particular match. It was common practice to invite and sometimes to hire, a noted cricketer from a neighbouring club. T. Green of Beverley seems to have been an occasional pro. and R. J. Miller, a Bridlington slow bowler, was expressly said to 'have acted as a professional' on occasions, which would seem to suggest that, at least in the 1860's, there was no great divide between amateur and professional.

Hull and Beverley could afford to employ noted cricketers, but little is known of the background of the professionals hired by the smaller clubs. The likelihood is that many were local and only semi-professional, supplementing their income by playing and coaching on a part-time basis. There is a possibility that T. Brown was a Skipsea cricketer and Hedon Wellington employed the Hull Kingston bowler, J. Mould, as their pro. in 1860. They were certainly not well paid and most of the clubs arranged a benefit match for them at the end of their engagement. J. W. Sagar of Bridlington received 30/- (£1.50) in gate money and subscriptions in 1867 from a game arranged against 'eleven visitors from the neighbourhood of Sheffield'. 30/- was about two weeks wages for a local labourer at the time.

Bowling analyses start to be recorded from time to time from 1867 in the form of balls, runs, maidens, wickets. These make it clear that six-ball overs were used and not the four-ball overs of the first-class game. Job Greenwood bowled '11 overs or 66 balls for 2 runs' in 1866 in a low scoring game against Malton. The average length of the very few innings that were recorded was 27 overs. Given the low scores of the period, many of the bowling returns must have been spectacular. Bowling figures begin to be recorded more frequently in Hull's matches after 1870.

The hours of play varied enormously. Beverley had a 9.30 start against Bridlington and a 10.30 start against Malton. 11.00 or 12.00 was more usual. A long, but undefined break for lunch and 'the usual interval' between innings seem to have been the norm, but stumps could be drawn at any time between 4.00 pm and 7.00 pm, depending upon the railway timetable. Hull scored 116 in 1857 and dismissed Gainsborough for 26. When they followed on and lost their first wicket without score, the visitors capitulated. 'It was arranged to play until 5.00 but at 4.00 the Gainsborough Gentlemen retired from the contest and handed over the ball'.

It was normal for both sides to provide an umpire. The way in which reports often comment that 'the umpire's decision having never once been called into question' suggests that this was not always the case. Four Driffield players left the field in 1872 in protest at 'the alleged unfairness of the Malton umpire'. A Hull St. George's player was criticised for 'giving way to such an extent to the violence of his feelings' when he was given out. Some games never got started. In 1830, 'the match between Bedale and Ripon did not come off, in consequence of the Ripon umpire pitching one of the wickets on uneven ground where it would have been impossible for the backstop to have turned the full balls of the Bedale bowlers'. When Hull United played Hedon, it had been agreed to draw stumps at 6.30 pm. With Hull needing 4 runs to win and the last man at the wicket, the Hedon umpire took off the bails. When the umpires arrived at the tent, they found a two minute difference between their watches. In the resulting dispute, the Hull club refused to hand the match ball over to Hedon.

Such disputes were not rare. The enthusiasm for placing bets on the results of matches can only have increased the pressure on the umpires from both players and spectators. One club was advised by the local paper, 'either to make a charge for admission or obtain the assistance of a policeman to keep the noisy element under control'. The umpire's decision may have been final but it was often questioned. Nevertheless it is quite clear that by 1870 cricket was being played enthusiastically throughout the East Riding.

Sources

[1] John Nyren. *The Young Cricketer's Tutor* 1833. Edited by C. C. Clarke 1974. Pages 46-52.

[2] Bowen pages 104-105.

[3] The teams are: Hull Town, Hull United, The Institute, Hull Zingari, Malton, Hedon, Beverley, Driffield, Bridlington, Hornsea, Londesborough, Pocklington, Kirkella and Flamborough.

[4] After the Second World War, Norman Pogson of Hull C.C. tried to reconstruct the averages for some of the early years by extrapolating the scores from match reports in the papers. They were printed in the Hull C.C. Year Books from 1945. These are useful in some ways, but can not give a full picture.

THE STRUCTURE OF
CRICKET IN A VICTORIAN TOWN
DRIFFIELD 1850-1900

All the local towns had established clubs in the 1850's, but it is unlikely that any one club can claim a continuous existence from that time. Before the advent of league cricket, club cricket was, in one sense, much less formal. Groups of like-minded individuals came together, hired a field, arranged fixtures almost casually and frequently played for more than one club in the same season. Usually they enjoyed a period of success before either waning enthusiasm, financial stress or the loss of the driving spirits, led them to wind up. Often a new club was formed almost immediately, assumed the old name, hired the same ground and had a nucleus of players from the defunct side.

The way in which clubs came and went may be seen most clearly in Driffield where, in October 1850, a match was played between 'six of the old club and eleven of the new club in a field off Scarborough Road'. Later a Driffield Club, said to be in the first year of practice, played Bridlington in 1855. One of the people connected with the formation of these early Driffield clubs was the Nottinghamshire and All England professional, Richard Daft. When he died in 1900, the Driffield paper published a piece recalling that Daft had been apprenticed to a local draper, Messrs. Robinson and Sons, and 'that he used to gather a few kindred spirits around him at 6.00 in the morning and practise in a small paddock on Beverley Road. He was also greatly instrumental in getting the first cricket ground laid'. Daft was born in 1836. If he served a seven year apprenticeship from 14 to 21, he would have been in Driffield between 1850 and 1857, which would be more likely to link him with the 1855 club than the 1850 one. He turned professional in 1858, presumably at the end of his apprenticeship. These Driffield connections help to explain his links with the Beverley Club, but his name does not appear in any of the early score-cards.

A study of the Driffield club in the 1860's and 1870's gives an insight into the way cricket developed in the Victorian towns. The

45

President was usually a local worthy of sufficient standing to bring prestige to the club. Christopher Sykes of Sledmere, E. D. Conyers, the commanding officer of the Driffield Volunteers and Reynard, a local J.P. all did a turn in office. T. R. Kirkby combined the positions of Secretary and Treasurer from 1855 until 1865 and 'was really the upholder of the club'. They were supported by a committee of eight.

It was traditional to begin the season with an internal club game between 'Marrieds' and 'Singles' or between the (first) eleven and a twenty-two (the rest). Such games give a chance to assess the size of the club and the nature of its membership. At a time when locally a labourer's wage was about 15/- a week, it was inevitable that a club which had a guinea subscription would draw its membership from a fairly narrow section of society. A guinea was felt to be too high in 1877 when the club was running into difficulties and it was reduced to 10/-, but the money was not the only limiting factor. Games were not played on one particular day of the week, indeed there are matches recorded on every day except Sunday. They often began in the morning or at noon, after a train journey to away games. These factors alone would prevent anyone in paid employment playing for the club. Thus out of a playing strength of about 35, they were all either men of independent means or small tradesmen and shopkeepers who could leave their apprentices to look after the shop. Ralph Teal, the captain for some of the period, had a china and glass shop in the town. Hewson, was, amongst other activities, a brewer. The Botterill brothers farmed at Garton. One interesting character was F. C. Matthews, who seems to have had the knack of getting himself invited to play in any match that was going on in the area. In between playing cricket, he was an agricultural chemist manufacturing animal feeds and fertilisers. Most teams could select a cricketing clergyman with time on his hands, who often proved to be one of the strongest players, having learned the game at public school and university. In Driffield's case, it was the Rev. Christopher Day.

The Junior clubs in the town were equally exclusive. After the last game of the season in 1861, about twenty of the Driffield Victoria Club adjourned to the Black Swan for some end of season celebrations, which ended with 'eight professional and promising young men' performing a quadrille. Their 'slight imperfections' and 'reeling propensities' were light-heartedly reported in the paper.

This drew an angry response from the club. 'The Victoria C.C. is composed almost entirely of young men who are apprentices or otherwise connected with respectable tradesmen in the town, who believing your report to be correct, have expressed themselves greatly displeased with them'. This drew a pointed retort from the editor that they were not apprentices 'but their own masters, or resolved to be on certain occasions'

In the 1860's Driffield played on a field in Shady Lane (Victoria Road) belonging to the landlord of the Falcon. They charged 3d admission for gentlemen but let the ladies in free, attracting sufficient numbers for Kirby, the landlord, to open a tea room on the ground in 1862 to provide refreshments. Lunch and tea for the teams was usually provided in a marquee erected on the ground, though they sometimes adjourned to the town centre, to the Falcon or the Bell, run by Kirby's wife. This could be a substantial meal such as the 'magnificent luncheon provided by Mrs. Kirby, which surpassed all previous spreads on similar occasions'. Such meals could hold up play for lengthy intervals! When Driffield played Heworth in 1877, the visitors were entertained to breakfast at the Bell, presumably because they would have made an exceptionally early start to reach Driffield, not the easiest journey in 1877. Such happenings added to the cost of membership and underlined the narrow social basis of the club. During the more prestigious games the town band played throughout the afternoon.

In 1866 the club moved to a ground 'adjoining King's Mill Lane' with 'an excellent view from the lane'. The precise position is not clear except that it was not the present ground. Since the landlord was Taylor, the present Taylor's Fields is a possible location. The reason for the move is not clear, but as they took supper at the Falcon after the first game, it is unlikely that there had been any dispute with Kirby. In any case they moved back to Shady Lane in 1867 before returning to King's Mill for the following season, but the high rent of £20 a year was to prove a constant problem.

Nevertheless they began to develop this ground in 1869, building 'a commodious and substantial pavilion' with money raised from supporters in the form of interest free loans. The 'substantial pavilion was only 12' x 9' with a wash basin and cold tap, fed from a water butt. The only fittings mentioned are nine drawers. A lean-to shed, 18' x 9' adjoined the pavilion to house the one-horse roller, but not the horse, which was presumably borrowed when needed. From

47

1860 the laws allowed the pitch to be rolled between innings, but whether such sophistication was common locally in 1869 is not certain. A 16″ lawn mower must have been for use on the wicket, for the rest of the ground must surely have been cut with a scythe. There is no mention of a groundsman, but it is almost certain that there was one. An iron telegraph stand and numbers, provided a primitive score-board and a flag flew proudly from the flagstaff on match days. The club also possessed two hand gates, presumably to control admission to the ground for those who had no wish to lean over the hedge to watch.

The length of the season was, to say the least, flexible. Clubs began to stir about Easter, but it was not unknown for the first game to be in June or even July. Free from any competition from football, the last game was nearly always in October. At first glance it is perhaps surprising that the harvest did not appear to have much effect, but the town clubs were not dominated by farmers and had no agricultural workers as members. Driffield did not play many fixtures in a season, six in 1865 and 1866, eight in 1868, plus a few internal club games. In most seasons they ran a 2nd Eleven. The railway system was the key to the fixture list, with games against Bridlington, Beverley and Malton, Hull and Scarborough all easily reached by train. Hornsea was a much more difficult journey, which probably explains why they were less frequently on the fixture list. The social prestige of a match at Tranby Croft ensured that the club made a special effort to overcome the transport difficulties involved.

Even a club that seemed as well established as Driffield led, in reality, an uncertain existence. They came close to folding up in 1860 because of the popularity of the Rifle Volunteers. Since the Riflemen paid for their own uniforms and, in the early days, their own weapons, it was inevitable that they would draw their recruits from the same narrow range of society as did the cricket club. Indeed the Government tended to see them as a bulwark against working class revolution. The two organisations were thus in direct competition for members, indeed the President of the club, E. D. Conyers, was the commanding officer of the Driffield Volunteers. There were many resignations from the cricket club in 1860, by men who had joined the Volunteers and found their new activities time consuming. The loss was such that the club had a long debate on whether to continue. It did so, but was clearly weakened.

Financially it existed on a hand to mouth basis. No A.G.M. ever

Ralph Teal. Right-arm under-arm bowler and Captain of Driffield in 1871.

reported a balance of £10 and the annual rent of £20 for the ground was a heavy burden. As a result 'matches had been few and far between' in 1873 since they could not afford to entertain many teams at the ground, nor pay something towards the rail fares for away games. Taylor would not reduce his rent and the club decided to fold, putting the pavilion and equipment up for sale by auction in order to repay their backers. Before the auction could take place, a hastily called public meeting in the town set up a 'provisional committee' for reforming the club. Driffield Town C.C., as it came to be called, survived, but went through a very lean period.

Its difficulties were increased by the formation of a new club, which came to rival it and then to replace it as the leading club in the town. 'Mr. Marshall's Cricket Club was formed on Tuesday and play has already commenced in a field belonging to the gentleman from whom the club derives its name, which is situated directly opposite the field of the Town Club'. A club (M.C.C.!) formed on Tuesday and playing on Saturday on a new ground, says much about the wickets of the period.

Henry Dickon Marshall owned the water driven corn mill at King's Mill. A prominent nonconformist in the town, he had been on the committee of Driffield Cricket Club, had stood for election to the local School Board and was prominent in public affairs in the town. When the Driffield club looked like folding in 1874, he immediately formed his own club, providing it with a field at a nominal rent, but stipulating that it was to be 'solely for young men connected with the Congregational Sunday School'. It is not clear if this restriction was in force for very long, but by 1877 they were running a 2nd eleven and had improved their fixture list to the point where they were playing the leading clubs of the area and were, clearly, the stronger of the two town sides. Relationships between the two do not seem to have been strained. They played each other and seem to have had members in common. Marshall's Club often played their more important fixtures on the town ground, which was certainly larger and probably remained in better condition. If they paid a hiring fee, the money was no doubt useful to the host club, which reported a £25 deficit at the end of the 1878 season at an A.G.M. to which only 8 members turned up. They survived until 1884 but could no longer claim any position of pre-eminence. At that date they were transformed into the Driffield Church Bible Class XI, playing their matches at Beechwood, the home of Canon

MATCHES FOR 1887.

MAY.
7th—Londesborough, at Londesborough.
14th—Hull Church Institute, at Beechwood, (Cup Tie.)
21st—East Hull, at Beechwood.
28th—Wetwang, at Wetwang.
30th—Marshall's, at Beechwood.

JUNE.
4th—Cup Tie (Second Round).
11th—Beverley & East Riding, at Beverley.
18th—Hunmanby, at Hunmanby.
22nd—Hull Police, at Hull.
25th—Middleton, at Beechwood.

JULY.
2nd—Londesborough, at Londesborough.
16th—Wetwang, at Beechwood.
23rd—Beverley United, at Beverley.
27th—Hunmanby, at Beechwood.
30th—Middleton at Middleton.

AUGUST.
6th—Hull Police, at Beechwood.
13th—Marshall's, at King's Mill.
20th—Beverley United, at Beechwood.
27th—Bridlington, at Bridlington.

SEPTEMBER.
3rd—Beverley & East Riding, at Beechwood.
10th—East Hull, at Hull.
17th—Bridlington, at Beechwood.

SECOND ELEVEN MATCHES.
May 21st—Langtoft, at Langtoft.
June 18th—Hull Rovers (2nd), at Beechwood.
July 9th—Marshall's (2nd), at King's Mill.
July 30th—Hull Rovers (2nd), at Hull.
Aug. 13th—Marshall's (2nd), at Beechwood
Aug. 27—Langtoft, at Beechwood.
Others may be arranged.

HONORARY MEMBERS.

MR. HY. BOTTERILL	MR. J. HOPPER
MR. H. BOTTERILL	MR. M. KIRKBY
MR. T. BOWMAN	MR. H. D. MARSHALL
DR. BRAND	MR. H. J. PARKER
MR. J. CONYERS	REV. G. PURCHAS
REV. CANON McCORMICK	REV. C. F. RAINSFORD
MR. R. DAVISON	MR. C. F SHARP
MR. W. DRINKROW	MR. SPENCER
MR. CRAWFORD EYRE	REV. R. WILSON
MR. F. FAWCETT	MR. W. WITTY
MR. W. FAWCETT	DR. WOOD
MAJOR HOLTBY	REV. R. WRANGHAM
MR. T. HOLTBY (Cowlam)	

MEMBERS.

T. ALLMAN	J. FOSTER	S. T. PATERSON
W. ALTON	H. GOODLASS	D. PINKNEY
G. BARKER	J. HARRISON	P. POOL
J. BARRETT	J. HOLIDAY	T. POOL
F. BERRY	H. JENNISON	E. RICHARLSON
J. BLACKBURN	C JOHNSON	A. SMITH
J. T. BROWN	J. KNIGHT	J. SMITH
G. BRYAN	GEO. LEASON	O. SMITHSON
M. DICKINSON	A. MC.LAURIE	J. SOKELL
H. DRY	E. NELSON	R. STEAD
B. ELLIOTT		

J. T. Brown's membership card for the Church Bible Class Cricket Club, Driffield 1887.

Newton, the Vicar of Driffield. The reasons for this metamorphosis, so typical of Victorian town clubs, were probably financial, as the new club was allowed the use of the ground free of charge.

Cricket flourished in the town in the 1870's in a variety of forms. The Driffield Victoria Club is best seen as a junior club making use of the ground on Shady Lane and playing evening matches (two innings) against opposition from both within the town and the villages. The Albert Club seems to have catered for youths. The private boarding and day schools in the town, particularly Monument House School and Firth's School in Shady Lane, played regularly. Both were exclusively middle class. Working class cricketers had more limited opportunities to play, but games were arranged between rival work places. The Victoria Iron Foundry played the St. George's Foundry, as did a team from the East Riding Linseed Cake Company against Matthew's Cake Mill. Nothing is known of the Union Jack Club which played at Wansford Road in the 1870's, nor of the Rising star and White Star teams which played several fixtures.

Given that in the 1871 census there were only 1041 males between the ages of 15 and 44 in Driffield, it is clear that a sizeable proportion of them played the game, but it seems probable that as in so many other aspects of Driffield life in the Victorian period, working class men would look towards the church and the chapel to provide a framework for social activities. Both Marshall's Club, with its nonconformist background, and the Church Bible Class side, opened their doors to a wider cross-section of society and offered the opportunity to play a reasonable standard of cricket against the best teams in the area. It was after all these two clubs which provided the opportunity for a future test cricketer to learn the game.

From time to time there were calls on them to amalgamate and in 1899 they did play a few matches as Driffield United against strong sides, but Marshall was a forceful character and his club remained a separate entity until his death in 1910 when the M.C.C. faded away. It was clearly subsidised and his heirs may not have taken such a benevolent view about it.

Two games in 1884 marked a significant advance for cricket in the town. The first, early in the season, was a match between Driffield and the Nondescripts, a strong side containing several pros. and H. Charlwood, a former Sussex county player who was with Scarborough. Faced with such unusually strong opposition,

Driffield hired George Ulyett, one of the most famous cricketers of the time to play for them in the match. Ulyett was Yorkshire's opening bat, renowned for his powerful hitting and regarded by Wisden as 'the best bat in the team and if he had not been able to get a run, he would have been worth his place for his bowling and fielding'. He was the first Englishman to get two fifties in a test match and, in the same year that he was at Driffield, took 7 for 36 in the Lord's Test v Australia. He made a big impression. 'Half a score of times at least the ball, sent flying out of the boundary by Ulyett, had to be hunted for in the long grass'.

That match was the catalyst for a much more ambitious scheme, 'the like of which had never been attempted before in Driffield', to stage a two-day game in August, involving many of the Yorkshire side. A special committee was formed to oversee the arrangements. The two 'Yorkshire Elevens' were to be captained by local men, J. T. Kirby and C. J. Young. Mrs. Kirby of the Bell was detailed to provide lunch at the ground at 2.00 pm. T. Shann, the groundsman, prepared a 'capital wicket' and the Driffield Musical Band was to play throughout the two days.

'At some considerable expense' the committee secured the services of a galaxy of stars. In addition to Ulyett, Kirby's side had the slow left armer, Ted Peate, a regular in the Test team and a Yorkshire bowler who took 1033 wickets at 13 a piece in his 8 seasons. The third pro. was Fred Lee, who had been in the County side for several seasons, but Kirby's side also contained the 'unadvertised' D. Hunter from Scarborough, who would have to wait a further four years before playing for Yorkshire. Once he made the breakthrough, replacing his brother, he remained the Yorkshire wicket-keeper for twenty-one years, keeping wicket to Hirst, Haigh and Rhodes.

Young's side included the brother, Joe Hunter, the current Yorkshire keeper and Test player. Louis Hall, Ulyett's opening partner for the County, was the anchor man, who acted as the natural foil for Ulyett's hitting. Hall incidentally was an occasional bowler with Yorkshire, who bowled either round-arms or lobs. The third star was advertised as 'J' Grimshaw, a misprint for Irwin Grimshaw, a regular County bat. In addition Young had the former Hull professional, Leonard Jackson. The committee hoped to pay for these men by a 6d gate.

After an initial set back, (the start of the game was delayed for an hour because of the late arrival of some of 'the cracks'), all went well. Young must have wondered what he let himself in for when he dropped Ulyett off a skier, but another local cricketer, the Rev. C. S. Smith, 'splendidly caught him with one hand at long off'. Kirby had a good game, scoring 25 and having match figures of 6 for 87 in 33 overs, whilst Young bowled his left armers reasonably tightly.

C. J. Young was to go on to have a distinguished career himself. He regularly topped the bowling averages for Marshall's, usually taking his wickets at an average of under 5 a piece. In 1888 he became the professional at Great Harwood in Lancashire, taking 7 for 40 against Padiham and 9 for 45 against Lowerhouse. This was before the start of the Lancashire League. He was back playing for Driffield between 1890 and 1892, but probably on J. T. Brown's recommendation, he was appointed to be one of the Halifax pros. in 1893, along with Brown himself when he was not required by Yorkshire. Again he was successful and became a much respected figure in the club, taking up the position of groundsman at the end of his playing career. There were very close links between Driffield and Halifax in the 1890's, when both Brown and Young often brought strong Halifax sides across the Pennines. Another Driffield cricketer, Alf Smith, was the pro. with the Scottish side, Cathcart in 1895 and with Bishop Auckland in 1896.

The Driffield Church Bible Class side disbanded in 1892, when their benefactor, Canon Newton, retired, forcing them to reconstitute the club on a more realistic financial basis. What emerged was a new Driffield Town Club, continuing to play at Beechwood, but without any links with the church. At the same time there was a strong movement to provide a ground in the town, which could house all the sports played in Driffield. A public meeting was told that all the suitable land was in the hands of Viscountess Downe, the lady of the manor, but she was willing to lease three meadows in King's Mill Lane for 14 years at a rent of £44 a year for the 11 acres. As a result a public company was set up, with 94 shareholders in the town purchasing 742 shares to provide the capital to create a Recreation Ground. By April 1893, at a cost of £513, a cricket square was laid with a boundary fence to separate it from the surrounding cycle track and a grandstand built from which spectators could watch both activities and the occasional athletics. One pleasant aspect of the original concept, which has continued in a different form to the present day, was the deliberate provision of an area where the town's children were allowed to play freely. Originally this was the north west corner of the ground on the present bowling greens. Two thousand people turned up on 8th July 1893 to see Harrison Holt open the ground and plant a commemorative oak tree.

Cycling, athletics and the Rugby Club moved happily into 'the Rec.' but Marshall's would not move and Driffield Town C.C. was extremely hesitant, which must have worried the shareholders since they had gone to the expense of laying out a cricket square. The Club's worry was that whilst they might attract better fixtures against such clubs as Pickering, they had to provide equipment for members and assist with train fares out of a subscription of 7/6d. a year. They would be faced with finding their share of the annual rent and the capital repayment. In the end they negotiated a fixed rent and a % of the gate receipts from matches to go to the parent body. The first cricket match on 'the Rec.' was played on 28th April 1894 against Hull 2nd XI and Driffield Town have played there ever since.

Their financial worries were to prove well founded. Despite an increase in membership from 87 in 1894 to 122 in 1896, they were faced with a financial deficit in 1895 of £10.4s.4d. and would meet increased costs because the first instalment on the cricket pavilion, built in 1895, would become due. They were also running three teams; a Friday Eleven, playing alongside the two Saturday sides. Their solution was not to raise subscriptions but to stop paying fares to away matches and to cut the wages of their professional from £30 a year to £20. Storer had served the club well for several seasons. His exact words are not recorded, but it is pleasant to see that Driffield had to do without a pro. in 1896. They had to increase the subs. to 10/6. in 1899 and did without a professional in 1900, but it was 1904 before they could announce a balance and move into a much more settled period in the history of cricket in the town, which has seen the Club progress into the Yorkshire League in 1995.

GRAND CRICKET MATCH AT DRIFFIELD.

FRIDAY AND SATURDAY NEXT, AUGUST 29th and 30th, 1884.

THE ABOVE MATCH BETWEEN

TWO ELEVENS OF YORKSHIRE

Will be played on the TOWN GROUND, KING'S MILL LANE,

When the following well-known Players will take part:

GEORGE ULLYETT,   E. PEATE,   J. GRIMSHAW,

F. LEE,   J. HUNTER,   W. BATES,

Of the Yorkshire County Eleven.   The remaining Players from the district.

AN EFFICIENT BAND IN ATTENDANCE.   LUNCHEON on the Ground at Two o'clock.

WICKETS PITCHED EACH DAY AT 11.30.

ADMISSION SIXPENCE.—Tickets may be had at Mr. Jackson's, *Times* Office, or of the *Express* Co.

H. A. PICKERING, } Hon.
J. T. KIRBY,   } Secs.

The first two day match at Driffield 1884.

CRICKET IN HULL

Much of the credit for the establishment of a major club in Hull belongs to Andrew Crossland, Hull's first professional. Born in 1817 at Dalton, near Huddersfield, he had had a distinguished first class career. 'He was regarded as Yorkshire's best bowler (right arm round) for many years and a batsman of great tenacity, once batting on a Hyde Park flier for 150 minutes to make 8 runs'.[1] He moved to Hull in 1853 where he quickly earned praise for 'the improvement which (his) tuition has effected in the Town Club'. By 1856 he was described as the present proprietor of the ground, which implied arranging the matches as well as organising the play. He carried out a major development programme, levelling out the ridge and furrow of the outfield and placing boundary flags to confine the spectators to certain areas. The markers had no cricketing significance, as all hits had to be run, including those into the crowd, which parted, usually, to let the fielder through. 'The newly erected Gothic dressing lodge' and a marquee for serving lunches added atmosphere to the ground, as did 'the recently formed band of the club', that played throughout most of the hours of play.

Crossland probably drew upon his contacts in the first class game to improve the fixture list. Two-day fixtures against the likes of York, Rotherham, Lincoln, Leeds and Newark were played between 1854 and 1856, which was a much more testing programme than the one Hull cricketers had previously faced. On the whole, Hull performed creditably, beating Lincoln and Rotherham by an innings, losing to York and drawing a rain abandoned match with Leeds. Stainsby scored the first century on the ground against Lincoln in 1856, 'a score very few cricketers will ever have the honour of obtaining' and 'the most brilliant ever seen played in Hull'.

The fixtures could be demanding in other ways. Even though the Victorians had the advantage of a cheap and efficient railway system, the two-day fixture against Newark meant crossing the Humber by the 6.00 am. ferry, catching the waiting train to Lincoln, meeting the connection for Newark in order to breakfast at the

Swan and Salmon at 8.30. Newark, with Tinley as their pro. scored 206 and dismissed Hull for 140 of which Crossland scored 98. Newark had reached 115 for 6 in their second innings, when the stumps were drawn at 3.45 pm to allow the visitors to return to Hull on the Friday evening. Such a programme would have been impossible for a working man and underlines the exclusive nature of the town clubs of that time.

The enthusiasm for the game spread outside the boundaries of Hull. On Thursday 5th July 1849, 'a cricket club (was) established at Hedon this evening to play in Mr. W. Tomlinson's field on the east side of Thorn Road'.[2] They held an end of season match between 'Town' and 'Country' members, which would indicate a flourishing club of at least a couple of dozen players. By 1850 it was called the Hedon and Holderness C.C. and was strong enough to play and beat a Hull Kingston side in 1851, which clearly rankled with the visitors. Whilst Hedon went to the Queen's Head for supper, 'the Hull gentlemen, apparently not relishing their defeat had supper provided at the King's Head Inn and left the town early'. By 1853 the club was known as Hedon Wellington and had fixtures against the Hull junior clubs and Kingston's second eleven. They developed a close relationship with Welton, playing a fixture against them in 1855 when they had Stainsby as their 'given man' and then, later in the season, combining to put out a joint eleven, again strengthened by Stainsby, to play the Hull first eleven. The area's growing strength in cricket terms, was confirmed in an exciting match in 1859 when a 22 of Hull bowled out the United Eleven of All England for 25 in their first innings, Crossland and Lee, the Leeds pro., doing the damage. The match ended in a tie.

The steady progress of the Hull Kingston Club under Crossland seems to have been checked in 1860 for reasons which are not at all clear. There is a period between 1860 and 1865 when it can not be confirmed that Crossland was Hull's professional or indeed that there was any pro. with the club. The game against the All England Eleven in 1859 was played on 'the new field of the Hull Club in Anlaby Road' at Argyle Street. When Hedon played a fixture against many of the leading players from Hull at Hedon in July 1860, the visitors, clearly a scratch side, called themselves Hull Zingari after the touring club formed in 1845. Moreover 'their bowling was rather loose.... most of the players not having been in the field before during this season, the original standard clubs being about defunct in Hull'. (There was, incidentally, a Beverley Zingari in 1864). Hull Kingston was playing fixtures again in 1860 and 1861, but they were against local sides, such as Burton Constable, Withernsea and Visitors; a far cry from York and Leeds. The obvious conclusion is that there was some rift between Crossland and the club in 1859. There is support for this view in the revival of the Hull Mechanics' Institute Club, which, originally founded in 1848, had folded in 1860. Despite its name it had a solid middle-class membership and when it was reformed in 1863, the names on the score-cards are mainly those who had played for Hull Kingston. In 1863, it was described as the strongest club in Hull. Crossland was an occasional pro. for Tranby Park in 1863 and when the All England Eleven made one of their visits to Hull in 1863, Crossland was not one of the four professionals chosen to play for the Hull 22.

Hedon Wellington continued to mature and develop as a club, no doubt helped by the occasional appointment of a professional. Copson in 1857, 'showed great agility and activity in the field' and was nicknamed 'the Indian Rubber Man'. J. Mould, the Hull bowler, was appointed in 1860. Stainsby played alongside Copson in 1857, which may suggest that he was not just 'a given man' but may have had some financial reward from the club. Parker, an Oxford blue, also played with Hedon in 1861.

By then Hedon Wellington had been in existence for at least twelve years, had had the benefit of professional coaching and had played against the better Hull sides. They may not have warranted a fixture against the Hull Town side of the late 1850's, but when they travelled to play Driffield in 1861, the fixture was clearly seen by the Wolds club as a severe test. The game was well advertised in advance. The match would start at 10.00, luncheon served at 1.00, ladies admitted free and gentlemen for 3d, all an indication of the importance with which the match was seen. In fact, it was 11.00 before the two captains tossed up and Driffield batted. 'After a few overs it became quite clear that the Driffield club would be worsted as the bowling and fielding of the other party was of such a first class style, which not only prevented the other side getting many notches, but stamped them as first class players'. Although 'overmatched' against 'powerful opponents' Driffield stuck to their task. 'Mr. Botterill made the largest score, but after adding 22 to his name, he struck at a ball that was cleverly caught at a long distance'. An under-hand bowler, one of the Ivesons, then cleaned up the Driffield innings for 53. Two Hedon wickets were captured before lunch, 'one of them being cleverly caught out by Mr. Teal, who although he fell and rolled over twice on the grass, never left his hold'. Torrential rain in the afternoon prevented the game being finished, but the match is interesting because of the clear sense of a pecking order in the local sides, which perhaps suggests that the Wold clubs had not developed as quickly as those around Hull.

Whatever was the cause of the rift at Hull Kingston, by 1865 matters were improving. Crossland can, with certainty be identified as the pro. in that year and the fixture list rapidly improved. A game against York, with George Freeman, saw the core of the former Hull side restored; Crossland, Terry, Twiss, together with J. W. Crossland and the Rev. C. Day. A match the following season against Malton however, showed how much ground Hull had lost. They were beaten by an innings and 34 runs by a Malton side containing Freeman, Dewse of York, the Rev. E. M. Cole and the ubiquitous F. C. Matthews of Driffield. It was after this game that Freeman was challenged by Terry to a single wicket match.

Crossland's links with Hull are less definite after these years. He was Beverley's professional in 1868, the Hull Mechanics' pro. in 1869. By then he was 52 years old and perhaps fading from the professional scene. In 1877 and 1878 he was playing for a junior side, Hull Criterion, alongside his sons. One of them, S. M. Crossland was a County wicket-keeper in the 1880's, deputising for Hunter in a few games. Andrew Crossland umpired for Hull occasionally in his seventies, reminiscing about 'the young Grace'. He died in 1902.

The Hull Mechanics', playing 'on the ground opposite the park, Beverley Road', remained a force in Hull cricket, enjoying some epic games against Sessay, at that time one of the more powerful sides in the North Riding. Indeed on two occasions they were actually billed as the North Riding. Hull can rarely have turned out a stronger side than for the second fixture in 1866 when they fielded no fewer than five sometime professionals in Green, Ullathorne, Job Greenwood, Crossland and Bearpark. Even so they were reduced to 19 for 7 in their second innings when stumps were drawn.

The fortunes of the Town Club were revived with the appointment of J. Wright 'one of the best professionals the Hull Club ever had the fortune to engage'. The improvement in the fixture list continued. The matches against Leeds, Grimsby and Scarborough were all lost in 1869, but they did represent the sort of

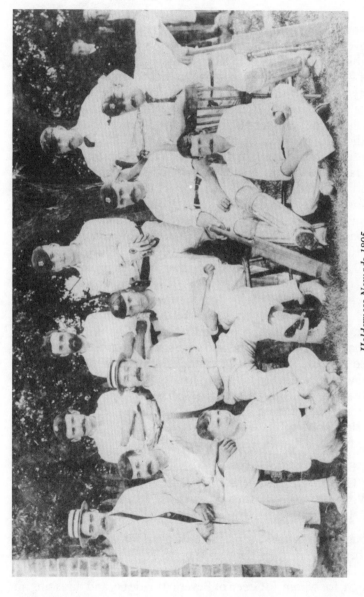

Holderness Nomads 1895
Back: C. Jordan (umpire), C. H. Fox (Hull), Rev. Goldsmith, A. K. Wilkinson, P. Frith. Middle: W. R. Smith,
J. W. Rome, H. S. Burstall (Hull), H. Bell (Hull), A. Siddall (Beverley). Front: H. Martin, F. Soulsby (Hornsea).

opponents that Hull ought to be facing and the most talented cricketers in the city were drawn back to the club.

J. Burman, a pro. from the Dewsbury area, was appointed in 1870 and given specific responsibility for preparing the wickets. The improvement in the batting performances over the next few years is probably attributable to the club's policy of appointing two pros. one of whom worked primarily on the wicket. Thus in 1871 Martin McIntyre from Nottingham was the 'cricketing' pro. and A. Constable 'the ground attendant and practice bowler' who 'earned the highest ecomiums for his preparation of wickets and tuition'. He was though, no mean performer on the field. It can be no coincidence that J. Smith scored 169 in 1870 and Lt. Hodder 203* in 1875, far and away the highest individual scores ever made on the ground. In the same year, 1875, Hull scored 357 against Scarborough's 217 and 62 for 3 in a two-day game. 636 runs was certainly the highest aggregate score on the ground by that date.

It was no doubt as a result of Burman's connections that Hull played an interesting match with the Savile Town Club of Dewsbury in 1870, for which 'Burman had prepared a very excellent wicket'. In a low scoring game, Dewsbury were 64 for 8 chasing Hull's 66. J. Cooke, 'a well known player late of Amcotts', who had joined the Hull club, was bowling 'very well and after a maiden he upset Hirst's wicket. The last man came in and Cooke availing himself of a new law, changed to the other end and with his fourth subsequent ball he bowled Watson. Cooke was carried to the pavilion shoulder height'. The new law in question allowed a bowler to change ends twice in a match and to bowl those overs consecutively. The Hull side, with Ullathorne outstanding, had 'fielded splendidly, especially to W. Lee's slow bowling'.

The bowlers' figures were:

J. Burman	6 overs	3 maidens	14 runs	2 wickets
J. Cooke	10 overs	5 maidens	13 runs	4 wickets
W. Lee	7 overs	0 maidens	18 runs	3 wickets
C. Ullathorne	3 overs	0 maidens	11 runs	0 wickets

Although it was a low scoring game, 26 overs for an innings seems to have been the norm for the period up to 1870.

Hull completed a satisfactory season by drawing with Scarborough, for whom T. Green of Beverley made 66, and thrashing an exceptionally strong Leeds side that contained five professionals in

Lee, Horsley, Barker, Baker and Brittain. It was in that match that J. Smith of Cambridge University scored his 169, containing two 5's and eight 4's out of a Hull total of 286. 'He was presented with talent money'. Hull had Allen Hill, the fast bowler who had replaced Freeman in the Yorkshire side, as one of their professionals in the match and bowled out Leeds for 85, of which Brittain made 52. The two seasons 1869-70 were clearly something of a watershed. The troubles of the early 1860's had been left behind and the club was re-established without question as the leading side in the Riding. They played 13 matches in 1870 but kept no permanent record of Saturday afternoon games. Of the nine 'games played with neighbouring elevens' that they chose to record they won 3, lost 2 and drew 4. They only played one second eleven match.

Over the next few seasons, Hull ventured into hitherto unexplored areas, the first ever matches against Keighley (with 6 pros.), Doncaster and, the only two-day game of the 1872 season, Boston. This match saw them facing Attenborough of Derbyshire and Seaton of Nottinghamshire. Their unaccustomed pace was such that 'when the Hull players went to the wicket, to use a vulgar but expressive term, an unmistakable funk was well established'. Durham, Otley, Sheffield Pitsmoor, Hunslet and Retford were added to the list by 1878. 2000 spectators turned up to see Hull defeated by an innings against Keighley and a 3-a-side single innings match was arranged to entertain the large crowd when the match finished early.

Hull was able to compete at this level reasonably successfully. From 1874 to 1886 they had, in Leonard Jackson from Derbyshire, an effective professional with an inclination to bowl 'head balls', presumably short-pitched bouncers rather than beamers. He was supported by a number of talented amateurs. Dennison took 5 wickets in 7 balls against Dewsbury and was 'presented with a new hat'. A. E. D. Harrison had two trials with the Yorkshire Colts in 1877 and eventually turned pro. with the Wakefield soap manufacturers, Hodgsons and Simpsons. J. Cooke was clearly an able player, but the bulk of the bowling was done by Jackson and L. W. Wallgate, who often bowled right through an innings. In 1876 their figures for the season were:

	Overs	Mdns	Runs	Wkts	Avge
L. Jackson	382.2	99	623	86	7.2
L. W. Wallgate	251.2	80	419	52	8.1

Between them they bowled only 3 wides and 7 no balls in the season. Both men scored centuries for Hull. Wallgate got into the Yorkshire side against Middlesex in 1877, but never quite made the standard. His career record of 9 runs in 3 innings and 1 wicket for 17 runs was disappointing. Charlie Ullathorne had a longer career with Yorkshire from 1868 to 1875, but his 283 runs in 38 innings was not such as to command a regular place. He was though an effective local pro. in the Riding, for Beverley in 1867 and for many of the other clubs on a match basis, a situation which allowed him to combine being the landlord of the White Hart in Silver Street with professional cricket. It is not always clear in these years whether he was being paid by Hull or whether he played as an amateur.

It is perhaps a sign of the growing maturity of the cricket scene in Hull, that the annual visits of the All England Eleven were beginning to pall. Matches against 22's often produced very dull cricket. The pick of the local cricketers were excellent fielders and it can not have been difficult for a seasoned professional like Lee of Leeds, bowling to a field of 22, to bowl 12 maidens in succession as he did in 1870. The reporter of the *Hull Advertiser* was certainly disillusioned at having to attend. He disliked 'the hideous looking pavilion belonging to the club'. The lunch interval of one hour was 'much too long'. The All England Eleven was 'a misnomer' as it contained far too many colts and even though 'Burman had prepared a very good wicket for the match' it was 'not of such first rate excellence as we have been in the habit of looking forward to, albeit it played very well'. He clearly didn't have a good day.

There was a general desire to try to do something different and better, which led to the Hull committee negotiating with Joe Rowbotham, the Yorkshire captain, and James Lillywhite of Surrey to stage a North v South match in 1875. This was almost certainly the first game in Hull to be staged between two elevens of first class players and, as such, was something of a milestone. There were the usual problems in trying to assemble stars from different counties. The three Nottinghamshire men, Richard Daft, Morley and Martin McIntyre did not play as advertised and the start was delayed until 1.30 pm on the first day because the South arrived by a later train than expected. Charlie Ullathorne and Leonard Jackson, the two Hull players were in the North's side. As with so many games in Hull over the years, the weather severely interrupted the match, but there was some good cricket in a low scoring game. W. G. Grace was dropped by Jackson early in his innings, at which 'the spectators manifested their gratification at the great batsman's good fortune'. He took advantage of the miss to put his first boundary hit out of the ground over long-on. It has to be said that in all the matches W. G. Grace played against local sides he had more than his share of good fortune. There is scarcely a report on a match in which he was not given several lives. The North lost by 23 runs, though the absence of the Lancashire opener, A. N. Hornby, who had scored 48 in the first innings, 'was much commented on'. He had left early to play in a match at Sunderland.

The match was a sufficient success to be thought worth repeating in 1876 and 1877. The 1876 game saw the marquees blown down by storm force winds, but W. G. Grace had a superb match, scoring 126 out of 159 in the first innings and 82 in the second. The Hull sectetary, G. J. A. Drake, had less to be pleased about, the rain and winds having a severe effect on the gate.

The 1877 match drew large crowds, 2000 on the Monday and more on the Tuesday, to see Lockwood, captaining the North, score a fine 103. W. G. Grace, dropped second ball, captained the South in a game they lost by an innings and 14 runs. The profits from these three games formed 'the nucleus of a fund for the promotion of cricket in the neighbourhood', though it is not known how the money was spent.

There can be little doubt of the enterprise of the Hull club in these years, but 1878 was to mark their most ambitious move, a three-day fixture against the Australians. D. W. Gregory's touring side had sensationally defeated a strong M.C.C. team in a single day by nine wickets, so it was not surprising that Hull was 'sneered at for presuming to play the Australian's level'. The original team contained four Hull players, but Ullathorne dropped out when he secured the catering contract for the White Hart. As is the wont in this kind of match, Barker of Scarborough, Platts and Mycroft of Derbyshire were also replaced from the original selection. Their places were taken by Rigley of Derbyshire, Greenwood of Yorkshire, McIntyre of Nottinghamshire and A. Wood, whose background is not known. Beverley, Scarborough and Malton each supplied a player, which with the three Hull men, gave the side a distinct East Yorkshire flavour.

4000 spectators crowded into the small Argyle St. ground on the Thursday morning to see 'Hull Town' score 250, with the Beverley

65

player Hasslewood Taylor making the top score of 53. Australia was in some difficulty, losing 6 wickets cheaply to the former Hull pro. McIntyre, Jackson and Wallgate. Of the top order, only Horan with 50 was able to make an impression, but Allan (78), Blackham (53) and Conway (46), batting at numbers eight, nine and ten, took the Australians to 305. Wallgate claimed 3 for 46 in 17 overs. 6000 spectators had attended on the second day. In Hull's second innings it was the fast-medium Boyle, rather than the 'demon' Spofforth, who destroyed the home side. He claimed 8 for 30 and Hull was dismissed for 68. The Australians won by 10 wickets, but batted on to entertain the crowd. It was a performance which reflected well on the standard of local cricket. Taylor went on to make 32 when a Scarborough and District side met the Australians. These two performances drew him to Yorkshire's attention.

It may well have been the large gate and the satisfactory way in which the game had been managed that drew Yorkshire to agree 'after some difficulty' to hold a county match against Surrey in Hull in 1879. Once again Hull's bad luck with the weather for important games continued. After weeks of continuous rain, no play was possible on Thursday and the match could not commence until 2.45 on the Friday, On what was obviously a difficult pitch, Allen Hill took 7 for 14 in 29 overs to bowl Surrey out for 50. Yorkshire, 55 for 1 at the close of the second day, struggled to 118 on the Saturday and then dismissed Surrey for 58 to win by an innings and 10 runs. There was every justification for pride in the success of the Hull Club during this period. They were drawing large crowds, were perfectly capable of staging prestige games and were able to play against the best of the club sides in the immediate region and beyond.

If Hull Town was the top of the pyramid, there was a secure base of junior clubs in the Hull area that supported them. The importance of Church and Chapel in the social life of Victorian times was reflected in their cricket teams. St. Paul's had been formed in 1868, the Church Institute on Spring Bank ran two elevens, whilst the Congos (Hessle Road Congregationalists) had fixtures against many of the leading club sides. Hull United, playing on Beverley Road in the 1860's, the North Eastern Railway Clerks, founded in 1873 and still a force in local cricket, Hull Criterion, which at various times had Ullathorne, C. Bearpark and Tony Crossland as professionals, all had fixture lists that took them out of the city and in to the Riding. Hull Police played other city forces such as Leeds

Hull Police and Prison Warders about 1905.

67

and Bradford., On the outskirts of Hull, villages such as Sutton, Hessle and Kirkella, were beginning to make the transition into club sides. Hedon C.C. continued to flourish with the frequent help of Hull 'cracks', but were reshaped in 1882 as South Holderness. They continued to play on the Sheriff's Highway ground and retained a close connection with the Iveson family. E. B. Kay was their first captain.

Two clubs that were to make a significant impact on East Riding cricket made a modest beginning in this period. Hymers played their first season in 1893 and soon attracted some good fixtures, although as essentially a school side, they were subject to frequent change and were something of an unknown quantity. Two of their early cricket coaches were Harrison and A. P. Charlesworth, the former Hull professional and Yorkshire player. Hull Zingari was declared to be 'a promising set' in 1896 under 'a capable captain, Askew' and so keen that they were said to be practising at 6.00 am which sounds to be at odds with the Zingari philosophy. They were strong enough to run two teams, but had a modest fixture list against Hessle, the Church Institute 2nds and Hymers. At one stage they were nicknamed the 'High Street Men' presumably because they had no ground of their own, but by the early 20th Century, 'the Gypsies' were playing at Newland. They had a number of advantages that almost guaranteed success. They attracted a prosperous membership and were financially secure; the Newland Orphanage and Cottage Homes benefiting in most years from the charity matches that they organised. They also developed a reputation for providing superior 'afternoon tea (which) still appears to be a feature with the Newland team' and of having a following that 'was distinctly classy. Interesting individuals brought in their train fair maidens, sumptuously and brilliantly arrayed and the vivid colours of their dresses, flitting hither and tither, formed one of the features of a pretty spectacle'. Attractive women and superior teas is a certain basis for success in any cricket club and it is not surprising that the Zingari fixture list steadily improved.

Welton had enough members to run a 2nd XI in 1878 but made little real impression on local cricket until the turn of the century, when under the patronage of their president Harrison-Broadley, they began to flourish. They were strengthened by an influx of new players when the Ferriby club disbanded and had strong links with F. S. Jackson, who played for the club from 1902 onwards when his

Ben Bolton
Yorkshire C.C.C., Hull C.C. and Hornsea C.C.

duties with England and Yorkshire permitted. A new pavilion was built in 1905, the outfield levelled and some 4 acres of the ground enclosed.

Given this kind of cricketing hinterland, it was to be expected that a talented supply of cricketers found their way into the Hull Club, where they benefited from the coaching. Ralph Crookes, who was one of the pros, from 1881 to 1884, was described as 'one of the best coaches in the county'. E. A. D. Harrison and 'Herbie' Hart both played for Yorkshire against Cheshire at Hull in 1887, Hart distinguishing himself by taking a hat-trick in the second innings, when he had an analysis of 29-12-47-5. He was in the full Yorkshire side that played Leicestershire later in the season, although that county was not regarded as first-class until 1895. B. C. Bolton played four matches for Yorkshire as an amateur between 1890 and 1891 claiming 27 wickets for 401 runs with his fast-medium bowling. He took 8 for 26 against Warwickshire, but that county also had to wait to receive first-class status. Bolton died in 1910 'after falling from an express train near Brough'.[3]

The fixture list continued to evolve. There was an interesting two-day game against Lascelles Hall in 1881, when the visitors arrived with names resonant of Yorkshire's early cricket, such as Thewlis, Lockwood, Bates and Eastwood. Todmordern was a regular fixture from 1882, whilst matches against Derby probably owed much to Leonard Jackson's links with that county. The Hull Town Grand Cricket Week was an innovation in June 1884, that saw games against Middlesbrough (two days), Hunslet, Pudsey and the Wakefield side Hodgsons and Simpsons.

'The Third Porters' as they were nick-named in the 1890s's had all the signs of a flourishing club, but their very success brought difficulties. The Argyle Street ground was widely perceived as being inadequate and it had long been felt that Hull was denied its share of county games because the ground was too, small to stage the matches properly. The Surrey game in 1879 had only been agreed with Yorkshire 'after some difficulty'. There was agitation to find a new ground throughout the 1880's, much of it undirected as when 'several enthusiastic cricketers have already hit upon a site for a first-class ground in Hull at Saner Lane'. By 1896 the issue could no longer be avoided. 'The Argyle Street ground is sinking and therefore will not last much longer without needing a considerable sum of money being spent on it'.

The Anlaby Road site, in use as a recreation ground, was purchased by the Hull Cricket Club Company Ltd., and the Circle constructed. Stoddart, the groundsman, began uprooting the Argyle Street wicket in September 1897 and had the new wicket laid down for the official opening on 7th May 1897. The Chairman, J. Downs, who had been associated with Hull cricket 'from the time when chimney pots were part of cricketers' wearing apparel' bowled the first ball on a very dead wicket, saturated by a week of rain; Hull's luck with the weather for important matches continuing. The visitors were Sheffield Pitsmoor, for whom Wainwright had a splendid match, scoring 36 out of a total of 50 and taking 8 wickets to dismiss Hull for 48. Despite the weather, 6000 spectators attended, producing a £60 gate. Downs reminisced that the first match at Argyle Street had resulted in a 9d gate.

With a new and impressive ground and a steady flow of talented cricketers into the team, the club must have felt that they could face the future with confidence. To some extent they were wrong, as cricket lost its way in the area and had to be reformed before the club's future could be secured, but the County did reward their enterprise in moving to the Circle. They were awarded Somerset in 1899 when Yorkshire, needing 23 to win, was denied victory by a thunderstorm. Hampshire was the fixture for 1900. Somerset and the South Africans played in 1904, Kent and Hampshire in 1905 and Hull came to regard two county matches a season as no more than their just deserts, so that the decision to allocate a solitary game against Leicestershire in 1907 was very badly received. There was always a degree of strain between Hull and the Yorkshire committee, which felt that the County Club had, proportionally, very few members from the Hull area and was therefore under little obligation to allocate county matches to the city. Toone, the Yorkshire Secretary, barely disguised this view in 1909. 'The County Committee must certainly be influenced by the appreciation shown in various districts and if Hull will show that appreciation, I am convinced that the Cricket Committee will not fail to reciprocate'. Hull could reasonably point out that they were isolated from the other county grounds and that members had fewer opportunities to benefit from membership than those in other areas, but such arguments carried little weight. One game a season created other difficulties. The club needed to make as much profit from the game as possible and 1/- to gain admission to see

Northamptonshire in 1909, not the most exciting of fixtures, drew adverse comments from local people, who were well aware that 6d was the normal admission for county games elsewhere. A sense of neglect by the county authorities was to be a recurrent theme in the city.

Sources:

[1] Hodgson p. 13
[2] Information supplied by Mr. M. T. Craven from the manuscript diary of James Iveson.
[3] A Woodhouse. *The History of Yorkshire County Cricket Club* 1989 p. 126.

CRICKET IN BEVERLEY 1840-1914

In one sense the prestige of the Beverley and East Riding Club cast a shadow over later Beverley sides. The Beverley Law Club founded in 1842, the Beverlac, the Amateur and the Britannia Clubs all playing in 1845, suffered by comparison and struggled to survive. Indeed when the Beverley Law Club was reformed in 1849 at the Holderness Hotel, it was reported that 'all the cricket clubs in Beverley have become extinct previous to the establishment of the present one'. Nevertheless, perhaps inspired by the visit of the All England Eleven to Hull in 1849, a Beverley Club was playing successfully in 1850 and won all their matches in 1851. Bickers, who had played in that match, was one of the leading players.

He was probably the man behind the move to bring back Clarke's tourists to Beverley in 1852. Sensibly the club hired a professional, Arnold of Cambridge, to help them prepare and approached two other professionals, Tinley of Newark and Wright of Sheffield, to play in the match itself. Staging the match on the Westwood presented its own difficulties, not least the virtual impossibility of enclosing 'the extensive flat on top of Beverley Westwood'. The club decided to make no charge for admission, but to rely on subscriptions to raise the £30 that was said to be needed, but it seems unlikely that that figure was the total expenses of paying Clarke and putting on the game.

The setting was very different from the grounds normally played upon by the professionals and was 'not altogether so good for cricketing as the All England men would have liked'. Hopefully, the livestock had been cleared from the area. On paper, the side was not as powerful as the one that had played in Hull, but the match was ruined as a spectacle by the weather. On the Monday, heavy rain delayed the start until the afternoon and 'sadly, spoiled the ground'. Conditions must have been difficult, for the All England Eleven were dismissed for 60. Tuesday was a beautiful day, the shops in Beverley declared a holiday and the townspeople walked up to Wreghitt's Mill (Black Mill) to listen to the military band and watch the local side get 82 in their first innings. The England Eleven were struggling at 33 for 6 at the end of the day. They were saved by the rain which prevented

73

any play on Wednesday, leaving Clarke and his party to catch an early train to Northampton for their next fixture on the following day.

After all the hard work that must have gone into arranging the match the outcome was disappointing, but the Beverley Town Club, as it was now called, enjoyed a successful period, including the defeat of 'Lincolnshire' by an innings in 1852, thanks largely to the bowling of Arnold and Bickers. By 1856 the local feeling was that the town would 'again rise to its former eminence' in the world of cricket, a mood that was further encouraged by the engagement of a left-arm professional, Kenyon, for 1857. Left-handed bowlers bowling round-arm, presented a very different line of attack to the normal one and it is clear that many opponents found him difficult to handle. 'Cricket has now become very popular in Beverley and the members of the Beverley and East Riding Club (sic) have spared no pains to make themselves proficient. The bowler who has been engaged, being master of his business, uses every means in his power to make the members good batsmen'.

It proved a false dawn. The club embarked on what looks like a prolonged period of internal bickering and mismanagement that was roundly condemned in the local paper. No games seem to have been played in 1858, though 'why there have been none this year, we are at a loss to imagine'. A new club, the Beverley Mechanics' (Institute) attracted many of the leading players and matters reached a climax in 1861 when in August, having lost every game, the club was slated in the press. 'Whatever the individual thinks of his own opinion, who has had the selection of these elevens which have been so disgracefully beaten in every contest in which they have been engaged... his ignorance has been conspicuous'. The individual who was singled out was Mr. Wreghitt, the owner of the mill and 'the manager of the Westwood matches'. If it was not enough to have the *Beverley Guardian* criticising him, Wreghitt's 'obstinacy' was soon being detailed in the *Hull Advertiser*, which reported that there was 'unpleasant feeling' between the Beverley and Hessle clubs. In a match on the Westwood, Hessle had, with Wreghitt's consent, strengthened their side with four players from the Hull Kingston Club. Having won the game, they expected to receive the ball, which was the normal practice of the time, but Wreghitt refused to hand it over, 'contrary to the law as per 'Lillywhite'... and this in opposition to the wishes of the majority of the Beverley side. However unless the ball be duly delivered up, the Hessle gentlemen have decided to

Cricket on Beverley Westwood about 1870.

decline playing the return or any future match under Mr. Wreghitt's management'.

Wreghitt was a character and like many 'characters' must have been difficult to live with. He was known as the Merry Miller because of his habit of descending from the mill during matches 'to favour the company with a few tunes on the Cornet'. A favourite was 'Oh dear what can the matter be', played as a batsman departed the scene and 'There's no place like home' when the visiting side lost. Rather surprisingly no one seems to have shown him an alternative way of blowing his trumpet.

One can sense the long shadow of the past hanging over the cricketers of 1861, when the *Guardian* continued its attack in a later edition. 'If cricket was carried out in Beverley as the Old England have done, by having a regular board of management, we might still have some good matches played, as it is well known that nearly all the old players, (who keep aloof solely on this account), would again join a club if properly managed'.

Perhaps the power of the press did have some effect. It was reported early in September that a match between the Town players and the Rifle Volunteers, an all-Beverley affair, 'was the very best match that has been played on the Westwood this year and we were glad to find amongst the players on both sides several of the old hands of the noted East Riding Club. Now that they have at last come to the rescue of the noble game, we trust we shall have a match every week, if amongst themselves, all the better when no disputes arise but those which may be readily settled'. The improved attitude was seen the following week against Hull United when 'the cricketers of Beverley were unanimous in coming forward to regain the laurels which had been lost so long'. A hint of the turbulence that had clearly been evident earlier in the season, came after the next match against Hull Kingston when both sides were congratulated on 'not a single word of dissatisfaction being expressed by either party during the whole day'.

Perhaps the storms of 1861 cleared the air, for a new club, Beverley Town Cricket Club, was formed in March 1862 with a committee of ten, plus officers. The subscription was fixed at 10/- and the playing strength was around 45 members in the early 1870's.[1] One club rule, perhaps the result of the troubled earlier period, was 'that every member shall be obedient to the captain of the game'. By 1874 they were renting 'the cottage and the tower', presumably as a store and changing room on the Westwood.

The story of cricket in the town for the rest of the period is peaceful and relatively straight forward, though it is perhaps only in 1869 that the Town Club was completely freed from the past, when a letter was received stating that an attempt to revive the Beverley and East Riding C.C. had been abandoned and that those concerned would give all the help they could to the existing Town Club.

Beverley was one of the first of the local clubs to employ a professional. The prosperity of the town, as opposed to the club, allowed them the luxury of paying for the pro. by opening a special fund (The Bowler's Fund) each season and inviting public subscriptions from gentlemen in and around the town. This enabled them to look wider afield than most of the other market towns and to draw on their links with Richard Daft, the Nottingham and All-England player, to obtain the services first of Hind and then of Parker, a Nottinghamshire colt. Hind's appointment was considered such a success that his original ten week contract was extended by a further six weeks. Caldecourt in 1865, Drake in 1866, future and past Yorkshire players such as Ullathorne and Crossland in 1867 and 1868, probably did much to raise the standard of cricket in the club. There are also signs of more care being taken to improve the wickets on the Westwood, as when 'Mr. Green prepared the wicket which played beautifully' against a Hull side which contained three professionals, Ullathorne, Clayton and Job Greenwood in 1868. The club was given a mowing machine in 1871, the same year that they acquired 'wing nets'. Such preparation of wickets was far removed from the earlier practice which left the choice of pitch to the umpires as long as it was within 30 yards of the centre of the ground.

In trying to compete against the best sides in the area Beverley could often find themselves out-gunned in terms of professional strength. They were badly beaten by York in 1868, but 'the professional element was so largely represented in the York XI that the match was played on very unequal terms and in our opinion, leaves the York men little room to boast of their success'. The score-card shows that York had four and possibly five professionals that day. A match against Hull Mechanics' the following season saw Beverley, without a pro., faced by Crossland, Drake and Ullathorne, who had just broken into the Yorkshire side. Ironically all three had been Beverley pros. in the past. One Beverley player, Dawson, took three hours over his 30 in that match and was rewarded with a new bat. The team also restricted Crossland to 12 overs without scoring, evidence perhaps of the rising standards in the club. Occasionally it would be agreed when the match was arranged that neither side would use professionals, but the agreement was not always observed. The start of a game against Hull Institute was held up for two hours in 1871 because the visitors arrived with J. Burman. Since he scored 0 and 1* when the match did eventually start, perhaps it was not worth making the fuss, but he did take 5 wickets and must have been impressive, because Beverley engaged him as their own pro. for the rest of the season, at a cost of £15.

Beverley was capable of displaying a certain panache in these years. Whereas most teams arrived at fixtures by courtesy of the N.E.R. and drew stumps in time to catch the train home, Beverley often arrived at away games in style. A party of twenty 'well-horsed and ably driven four-in-hand by the spirited proprietor of the Beverley Arms' arrived to play Hornsea in 1869, whilst 'the distant sound of a (post) horn early in the morning warned the peaceful inhabitants of Sleepy Hollow' that the Beverley side was arriving to do battle with Hedon.

A further sign that the standard of cricket was rising within the club was the selection of one of its members for Yorkshire. Hasslewood Taylor had played for the East Riding in 1874 as part of Lord Londesborough's attempt to form the breakaway Yorkshire United County Club. He had not impressed, but in 1878 he opened for a Hull Select eleven against the Australian tourists and top-scored with 53 against a very strong attack. It was no doubt this performance that persuaded Yorkshire to look at him in 1879, but his county record of 36 runs in 5 innings would seem to suggest that he was some way short of the necessary standard.

Cricket in the town was in a very healthy state in the 1880's with a number of successful junior clubs sharing the Westwood. Beverley Old Foundry played against various Hull sides such as South Myton, the Railway Clerks, Southcoates and Hull Dock Offices. Beverley United had a more ambitious fixture list against the Driffield sides and Hessle. Their crowning achievement came in 1886 when they won the Alderman Leake Knock-out Cup by defeating the Hull Second Eleven by 5 wickets in a two innings game. When they returned to Beverley by the 7.45 train, there was a brass band waiting to escort them through the streets. They were hoisted into a waggonette by a crowd, which then removed the horses and pulled them in triumph through the streets to the Beverley Arms, where the captain made his speech. The team then made their way via the Holderness Hotel to the Club's headquarters at the Dog and Duck, 'the evening being spent in conviviality'.

There was a significant development in 1884, when after well over a hundred years of playing cricket on the Westwood, the town's premier side moved to a new ground. There was a fashion at the time for establishing Recreation Grounds where various sports, especially cycling and athletics, could be staged on a commercial basis. An entrepreneur in Beverley bought four acres in Wilbert Lane, (near the present Swimming Pool), which had been the old Iron and Waggon Works and laid down a pitch surrounded by a cycle and athletic track. Since the ground was walled, it had the advantage over the Westwood that admission could be easily controlled and the resulting 'gate' used by the club. The new ground was played on for the first time in August 1884 when the professional's benefit match was staged there. It 'seemed to cause no little surprise to the cricketers and spectators by the satisfactory way in which the wicket played'. Beverley Town moved all their matches to Wilbert Lane for the following season, though the junior clubs continued to play on the Westwood.

The ground was on the small side. The cycle track was only a fifth of a mile in circumference and the combination of good wickets and short boundaries produced some high scores. T. Pride of York, who had a few games as Yorkshire's wicket-keeper in 1887 before David Hunter replaced him, scored 201 against Beverley in 1894. The following year the Yorkshire Gentlemen, who 'turned up late and short-handed as usual' so that no play was possible until after lunch, found themselves chasing a Beverley total of 373 and were reduced to 15 for 4 when stumps were drawn. Not all the bowlers found the wickets unhelpful. When Londesborough Park was building up a large score in 1894, W. H. Anstead went on to bowl. From other reports it would seem Anstead was one of the older players in the team, but 'his peculiar under-hand twisters puzzled the batsmen to such an extent that 5 wickets fell to him for only 13 runs'. This is the last specific reference to under-hand bowling noted and Anstead was not a regular bowler for the club, but the tone of the report is not such as to suggest undue surprise at someone bowling under-hand.

Beverley was very successful in 1895 remaining unbeaten throughout the season, though Driffield complained bitterly that they had failed to turn up for their match because several of the best players were assisting Hull. They demanded compensation for the expenses involved and for the loss of gate money. Beverley could attract large gates to the Recreation Ground. A thousand people attended to see Beverley play J.J. Harrison's Eleven (of Brandesburton Hall) in 1895 when Lord Hawke and F. S. Jackson were in the invitation side. Despite this the move to the Recreation Ground increased the financial difficulties that the club had hinted at in 1883. Then they had remained solvent only because of the generosity of a number of wealthy patrons, who were prepared to bail them out of trouble at the end of each season. In 1885 they had accepted the tenancy of the Recreation Ground at £40 a year and had been able to sub-let the cycle track for £25, but in 1891 the rent had been raised to £66.15s.0d. plus rates and taxes. This meant that the club had built up a deficit, which was increasing by about £30 each year. A Special General Meeting in 1896 considered relinquishing the tenancy, but there was no alternative ground available and not enough financial backing to think of buying land.

The decision was forced on them in 1908 when the club faced the prospect of being without a pitch for the following season, after the owners of the Wilbert Lane ground sold it for building plots. They were saved by the generosity of J. A. Dunkerly, a former captain of the club, who purchased five acres of unpromising land at Norwood and hired workmen over the winter to level out, under the supervision of Hull C.C.'s groundsman, the ridge and furrow, traces of which can still be seen on the third team pitch. When the ground was opened on 22nd May 1909, not only had a drainage system been installed and a wicket laid that was fit to be played on, but the brick pavilion had been built with two changing rooms, a central dining area and a score-box upstairs. A Grandstand, planned for the opposite side of the ground to the pavilion, never materialised. The ground was bounded by wooden rails and a grass cycle track. The bowls section played on the outfield in front of the pavilion. All had been achieved at Dunkerly's expense and was leased to the Beverley Town Cricket, Bowling and Athletic Club for a nominal rent.

One feature of Beverley cricket in these years is the service of two of their professionals. From 1880 onwards, the club tended to retain their professionals for three or four seasons. As with most clubs they tended to choose a bowler, who was expected to tie up one end and often ended up bowling nearly half the overs delivered in any one season. An ability with the bat was seen as a bonus rather than an essential. For four seasons from 1887 the pro. was T. Wardell, who was a model of consistency. His figures are only available for three of these seasons, but in those he took 248 wickets at 6.2 each. In 1892 however, Beverley appointed J. C. H. Mitchell from the Huddersfield area, who was to remain the pro. for the next fourteen seasons. He settled in Beverley opening a sports and tobacconist shop in Toll Gavel. He was a useful bat, who scored in the region of 500 runs a season, despite the tendency of amateur captains to move him up and down the order from opener to number eleven. He achieved the double of a 1000 runs and a hundred wickets in 1901, but over the years it was his bowling that stood out. His full figures are only available for nine of the fourteen seasons, but in five of those he took 100 wickets. His full figures for those nine seasons are:

3232 overs, 835 mds, 6592 runs, 858 wkts, 7.6 avge

Between 1906 and 1911, probably because of the financial pressures on the club, Beverley did not appoint a professional. Given his record, there is little doubt that Mitchell could have found a position with several of the neighbouring clubs, but he stayed on to play as an amateur and was, rather unusually, granted a benefit match in 1906, which perhaps confirms that it was finance that had prevented the club retaining him professionally. As an amateur, he became the regular opening bat and scored plenty of runs, but it was his bowling that dominated. The figures are available for 15 of the 23 seasons between 1892 and 1914. They are:

5542 overs, 1275 mds, 15914 runs, 1366 wkts, 11.7 avge.

It is probable that he took 2000 wickets for Beverley in 23 seasons. He must occasionally have permitted himself a wry smile in 1912 when J. T. Green of Thornton Dale was appointed the club's professional. No doubt Green, who proved a competent and successful bowler, was secured for a smaller salary than Mitchell would have expected, but Mitchell continued to tie up 'his' end and bat high in the order until the outbreak of the war. The plaque in his memory on the side of Beverley's score-box reads:

In memory of
Charles Hartley
Mitchell
Cricket Professional
1892-1905
A True Sportsman
One of the best

Sources:
[1]   H. C. R. O. DDBD/5/146-150.

WOLDS CRICKET AND LORD LONDESBOROUGH

William Henry Forester Denison, 2nd Lord Londesborough in 1860 and Earl of Londesborough in 1887 was the second largest landowner in the East Riding after Sir Tatton Sykes. He owned 33,000 acres in the Riding and a further 20,000 in the North and West Ridings that gave him an income of £70,000 a year in 1873.[1] It is not surprising that he could 'feel superbly feudal' on occasion. In addition he had £2,000,000 in stocks and shares. It was a vast fortune and as one of his relations said, he 'set himself to its dispersal, itself the work of a lifetime, with zest and abandon'. He was a close friend of Edward, Prince of Wales, whose visits to Londesborough Park and Londesborough Lodge in Scarborough caused much local excitement, even if the drains at the Lodge nearly caused his death from enteric fever in 1871.

There is no doubt of Londesborough's genuine enthusiasm for cricket. He was a patron of the County Club, sponsoring two matches against Middlesex in 1874, and, much more significantly, was one of the major forces behind the Scarborough Festival. He became the President of the M.C.C. in 1876 and regularly attended the matches at Lords. He seems to have been popular with the cricketers with whom he came in contact. Louis Hall, the Yorkshire opener, named his children after the Earl and his wife. 'His generosity to old professionals was legendary. He offered to pay for specialist treatment for Harry Dewse's battered hands. Said Dewse: "When I found it would cost him £50 and as I had no pain, I declined to go"[2]

His enthusiasm for the game at the time that county cricket was evolving led him into a situation that was potentially damaging. In January 1863 a meeting at Sheffield had resolved 'that a County Club be formed'. There were those who would have preferred to see cricket in the county develop under a different, more patrician leadership, than those of the manufacturing classes of South Yorkshire. In the same year, 1863, a group of prominent gentlemen met at Harker's Hotel in York and decided to create a County Club, 'it having been the desire for several years of many gentlemen in

Yorkshire to have the County well and thoroughly represented in the cricket field in what might be termed county matches and also in gentlemen's county matches'. The distinction is revealing of their thinking. The meeting chaired by the Hon. G. E. Lascelles, elected Earl Fitzwilliam as President and had the support of Lords Londesborough, Feversham and Wenlock.

The County Club never materialised, but the Yorkshire Gentlemen's club was established and was to have a significant input. Based on York, some distance from the industrial heartland of Yorkshire cricket, their select membership represented an amateur tradition that was sometimes to lead to tensions with the more professionally orientated County committee. The Yorkshire Secretary opposed the inclusion of a representative from the Yorkshire Gentlemen on an enlarged committee in 1882 on the grounds that 'they wanted to have all games at York, at the expense of everywhere'.[3]

In 1863 Yorkshire County cricket was still in a formative stage and Londesborough's participation in the creation of a rival body can be understood, but his role in the manoeuvring of 1874 must call his judgement in to question. At the end of the 1873 season various groups who were united in their dislike of Sheffield's dominance of Yorkshire cricket, met at the Talbot Hotel, Malton 'for the purpose of bringing before the public a scheme for the formation of a new county cricket club for the North and East Ridings'.[4] A second meeting at York decided on the title 'Yorkshire United County Club' and Londesborough was invited to become the President. The new committee met at Abbott's Railway Hotel in York. The representatives were mainly from the North and East Ridings and included Hull, Hornsea, Malton, Scarborough and York. They decided on 'the formation of a County Cricket club upon the basis of a thorough representation of cricketing promise and talent in good cricket matches'.[5] Until there is a full scale biography of Lord Londesborough, his motives must remain open to debate, but the desire of a very rich enthusiast to have a county side of his own, must be considered.

The project was not necessarily doomed to failure. County fixtures did not crowd the season and the established county players were not adverse to engagements between matches. Roger Iddison, who acted as the Assistant Secretary, was an experienced 'fixer' who had the necessary contacts with the professionals to obtain their services. Iddison, Yorkshire's first captain, was well aware of the commercial opportunities that existed for professional cricketers to market their skills.

The first match of the newly formed Yorkshire United County Club, a trial between the North and East Ridings, was played in Hull in May 1874, its purpose was presumably to see which local players were suitable for the six 'county' matches played later that year against Lancashire, Harrow Wanderers, Derbyshire (2) and Durham (2). Roger Iddison captained the North Riding, J. Cooke, the Hull bowler, the East Riding. The eleven players selected for the East Riding are an interesting reflection on the strength of the clubs. Cooke, Hearfield, Jackson, Wallgate, Ullathorne, Drake (all Hull), Taylor (Beverley), Bosomworth (Malton), Wade (Hornsea), Storey (Warter) and Leatham (Wakefield). Four were to play for the official County but none of them became established players in the Yorkshire side, which is probably a realistic indication of the strength of the Yorkshire United Club.

The match did arouse the interest of the Hull public and there was a large attendance on the Saturday. Hasslewood Taylor's fielding ability as a specialist longstop, was again noteworthy. 'The first bye was noted with the score at 65, Mr. Taylor's longstopping having hitherto prevented extras'. The Hull favourite, Charlie Ullathorne hit one of Reynolds 'head balls' clean out of the ground and carried his bat in the first innings. The score-card for the match was:

THE NORTH RIDING:

J. Hicks	lbw	b Wallgate	8	b Bosomworth	25
J. Easby	c Drake	b Jackson	12	b Bosomworth	0
H. Reynolds		b Cooke	18	b Jackson	0
T. Emmett		b Cooke	28	c Ullathorne b Bosomworth	8
R. Baker	c Storey	b Cooke	1	not out	27
H. Tiplady		b Bosomworth	3	c Leatham b Bosomworth	3
J. Todd	c Jackson	b Cooke	7	b Bosomworth	0
H. Graves		b Cooke	0	c Wade b Cooke	3
H. Nixon		not out	4	b Bosomworth	3
R. Iddison		b Bosomworth	0	c and b Cooke	1
G. Anderson	c Wallgate	b Cooke	8	b Bosomworth	10
		Extras	7	Extras	0
			96		80

84

EAST RIDING:

G.J.A. Drake		b Reynolds	8	b Tiplady	23
C. Ullathorne		not out	17	c and b Tiplady	4
H. Taylor		b Reynolds	0	b Emmett	0
E. Bosom-worth	c Anderson	b Emmett	1	b Tiplady	7
L.W. Wallgate	c Reynolds	b Emmett	0	b Reynolds	3
L. Jackson		b Reynolds	4	run out	3
D. Hearfield		b Reynolds	0	b Reynolds	4
G.A.B. Leatham	c Todd	b Reynolds	0	b Reynolds	0
J. Cooke	c Baker	b Reynolds	0	not out	2
R.J. Wade	c Anderson	b Reynolds	5	b Reynolds	1
J. Storey	c Graves	b Reynolds	0	b Reynolds	1
		Extras	4	Extras	4
			39		52

The club played seven matches against '22's' in 1875, a 'county' match against Hampshire in 1876, when Dewse took 5 for 9, but folded after one match in 1877. None of their matches was regarded as first class.

In 1884 a North Riding of Yorkshire C.C. was formed, which by 1888 had evolved in to the North and East Ridings of Yorkshire C.C.. Londesborough was their President in 1889 and Lord Derwent in 1890. There was no apparent animosity with the Yorkshire authorities. There was little to be gained by crossing as powerful a figure as Lord Londesborough and it is probable that the clubs were not perceived as 'county' in any meaningful way. When the full Yorkshire side played the North Riding C.C. in 1884, the scores were Yorkshire 530, the N.R.C.C. 162 and 41 for 3.

It comes as no surprise to find that Lord Londesborough encouraged cricket on his estate. He instituted a Cricket Carnival in 1884, when 'strengthened by several gentlemen from M.C.C.', Londesborough Park defeated a strong York side. Later in the week they defeated Marshall's Club with the Leeds professional Saul Wade, supporting the Park pro. Alan Siddall. The following year the Carnival became a Festival in which 'Lord and Lady Londesborough visited the ground each day'. It included a two day game against a Beverley and East Riding side. Perhaps the Londesborough

Festival was the germ of a much larger idea, the Scarborough Festival, though there had been a nine day cricket carnival in the town in 1876.

There is no way of knowing how long cricket has been played at Park Farm, Londesborough, but it has almost certainly the longest history of continuous use as a cricket ground in the Riding. It predates the Earl's time and as there is no reason to presume that the 'Railway King', George Hudson had enough time or interest to establish a cricket ground when he owned the estate, the most likely beginnings are under the Duke of Devonshire in the early 19th Century. That can be no more than speculation until new evidence is found. The earliest record of a match is no earlier than 1857 and claims for fixtures dating back to 1820 do not seem to have been substantiated.

Market Weighton had a cricket club in 1852 when they played Howden, a fixture which was repeated the following season. Interestingly a joint Market Weighton—Londesborough side played Etton at the Park in 1857 which is open to the interpretation that Londesborough was not well enough established to face Etton on its own. In the same season, Market Weighton played Etton at Londesborough but by 1863 they had their own ground and were well enough established to engage Osborne from York and Crossland from Hull as match professionals for some fixtures. The following season they engaged Lister as the club professional, defeating Beverley on a sporting wicket on which 'the balls bumped and fluked considerably'.

There is a dearth of information on Pocklington for a number of years after Charles Cartman and Leonard Hobson played their single wicket match on the West Green in 1843. In 1850 Pocklington School played Beverley Grammar School 'on the Pocklington new ground', but it is not clear whether the new ground belonged to the school or to a town club. Both headmasters played in the fixture, which was itself a return match of a game played the previous year. When 11 Gentlemen of Pocklington played 11 Gentlemen of Beverley in 1857, the heads were not playing, but both Rev. F. Gruggen and Rev. G. Gruggen appear in several Pocklington C.C. sides in the 1860's and it is likely that a strong link existed between club and school. Pocklington did not develop in to one of the stronger sides and suffered a crushing defeat by Malton in 1871. Acknowledged to be the strongest side in

86

LIST OF MATCHES.

DATE.	DAY.	CLUBS.	GROUND.	RESULT.
May 7	Monday	Married v. Single	Mkt. Weighton	
" 14	Monday	First Eleven v. Hull Criterion	Mkt. Weighton	
" 15	Tuesday			
" 21	Monday	First Eleven v. Hull Town 2nd	Hull	
" 22	Tuesday	Second Eleven v. North Cave	North Cave	
" 28	Monday	First Eleven v. Brayton	Brayton	
June 2	Saturday	First Eleven v. 15th Regiment	Mkt. Weighton	
" 7	Thursday	Second Eleven v. Newbald	Mkt. Weighton	
" 16	Saturday	First Eleven v. South Cave	South Cave	
" 21	Thursday	2nd Eleven v. Pocklington Grammar School	Shipton	
" 26	Tuesday	Second Eleven v. North Cave	Mkt. Weighton	
July 2	Monday	First Eleven v. Cherry Burton	Mkt. Weighton	
" 7	Saturday	First Eleven v. Hull Criterion	Hull	
" 12	Thursday	First Eleven v. Pocklington Grammar School	Shipton	
" 19	Thursday	Second Eleven v. Newbald	Newbald	
" 30	Monday	First Eleven v. Cherry Burton	Cherry Burton	
Aug. 4	Saturday	First Eleven v. Hull Town 2nd	Mkt. Weighton	
" 13	Monday	First Eleven v. Brayton	Mkt. Weighton	
" 20	Monday	First Eleven v. 15th Regiment	Beverley	
" 25	Saturday	First Eleven v. South Cave	Mkt. Weighton	
Sept. 3	Monday	Second Eleven v. Mr. Buttle's Eleven	Shipton	
" 10	Monday			

Market Weighton Town C.C. membership card 1883.

87

the region and 'the metropolis of cricket in the County of York', Malton scored 205 and dismissed Pocklington for 25 in each innings, the bowling of Bosomworth and Brown proving too professional for the local side.

Once Lord Londesborough inherited the estate in 1860, the Londesborough Park Club could no longer be seen as a village side, but the element of country house cricket was not all pervasive. The club drew players from quite a wide area and provided opportunities for guests at the Hall to play against sides from the surrounding town clubs. In some ways Cherry Burton functioned in a similar way under the patronage of the Burton family. They had a professional by 1862, presumably engaged by Lord Londesborough to act as a coach and net bowler to his family. 'The peculiar left-arm bowling of Mr. Heseltine on the Londesborough side' proved too much for the Driffield club in both matches that season. Those Londesborough teams included Usher, Stephenson and Musgrave, names which had previously appeared in Market Weighton sides.

They also contained an Egerton. The relationship between Capt. Egerton and Lord Londesborough is not known, but most country house cricket at the Park in the 1860's centres around him. When Brantinghamthorpe played at Londesborough no less than four members of the family played for Cpt. Egerton's Eleven. In 1868 when Beverley played at the Park it was against Egerton's XI, assisted by Ullathorne, who had been brought in as the match pro. to support Coxen, the club professional that year. Lord Londesborough's XI is a much less common occurence in these years. Egerton was to be prominent in local cricket until 1871 when it was announced that 'Major Egerton was leaving Londesborough for the south'.

Lord Muncaster took an interest in cricket at Warter, where the estate side was often described as Lord Muncaster's XI. They played a two day game in 1870, complete with the band of the Pocklington Volunteers, against Usher's XI. At least four members of that family were prominent in local cricket in the 1880's, W. A. Usher being good enough to be considered by Yorkshire in 1887. Alongside E. W. Usher he was a mainstay of the Londesborough Park sides of the 1880's. E. and H. Usher were playing a little earlier.

The Market Weighton Club seems to have been firmly established with a fixture list that marked it out as one of the more successful junior clubs in the area. In 1883 with Lord Londesborough, Lord

Herries, Col. Harrison-Broadley and other local worthies as patrons, it was strong enough to run a second eleven. The first team, captained by R. Newbald, played from May until the end of October with home and away fixtures against Brayton, Cherry Burton, Pocklington School, South Cave, the 15th Regiment stationed at Beverley, Hull Criterion and Hull 2nd Eleven. They seem to have called in Siddall and two of the Ushers on a fairly regular basis for their tougher games, but they were certainly strong enough to hold their own, scoring 231 against Hull in 1884 and restricting their opponents to 129 for 7. Howden C.C. and Beverley were on the 1884 fixture list. The club was still in existence in 1908.

Like most Victorian clubs Pocklington had its crises, when the management of the club collapsed or they lost their ground. After playing uneventfully in the early 1890's the club folded. 1895 was a barren year. 'There is abundance of material for a capital cricket

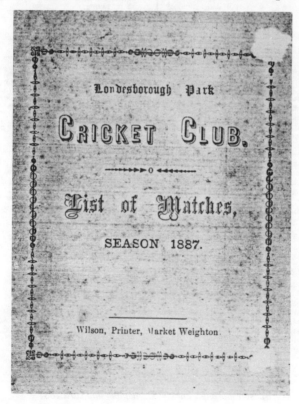

Londesborough Park
CRICKET CLUB.
List of Matches,
SEASON 1887.
Wilson, Printer, Market Weighton.

1887

Londesborough Park Cricket Club

PRESIDENT:

THE RIGHT HON. LORD LONDESBOROUGH.

PATRONS:

The Hon. W. F. H. Denison,
Sir Philip Egerton, Bart.
Christopher Sykes Esq., M.P.

Arthur Duncombe Esq., M.P.
The Rev. R. Wilton, M.A.
Lieut. Colonel Young.

CAPTAIN:

G. COBB.

COMMITTEE:

G. Cobb,
H. Usher,
W. A. Usher,

H. B. Young,
R. R. Young,
J. Wreghitt.

HON. TREASURER:
H. B. YOUNG.

HON. SECRETARY:
R. R. YOUNG.

LIST OF MATCHES.

DATE		CLUB	WHERE PLAYED.
Sat. 7th	May	Driffield Church 89 *bm*	Londesborough. 56/or 4
Sat. 14th	,,		
Sat. 21st	,,	Holme 59. *Lost*	Holme — 46
Sat. 28th	,,	Beverley and East Riding 40 *los*	Londesborough. 106
Mon. 30th	,,		
Sat. 4th	June		
Tues, 7th	,,	S. Peter's School 59 for 9 B.	York — 192
Sat. 11th	,,	Driffield Marshall's 8 for 7 w 3s.	Londesborough. 122
Tues. 14th	,,	Yorkshire Gentlemen s4 60 W m.	Londesborough. 147
Sat. 18th	,,	Holme 111 lost.	Londesborough. 69
Mon. 20th	,,	York 167 lost.	York — 74
Fri. 24th	,,	Hunmanby Mitford 152 Lost.	Londesborough. 58
Sat. 2nd	July	Driffield Church 47 Won.	Londesborongh. 82
Tues. 5th	,,	Yorkshire Gentlemen 70 6 B.	York. — 166
Sat. 9th	,,	S. Peter's School	Londesborough.
Sat. 16th	,,	Colonel Brooksbank's XII won	Middleton. — 122
Mon. 18th	,,	York 70 won.	Londesborough. 179
Sat. 23rd	,,	Driffield Marshall's	Londesborough.
Sat. 30th	,,	Primrose League won	
Mon 1st	Aug.		
Sat. 6th	,,	Beverley and East Riding	Beverley.
Thurs. 11th	,,	Mr. Bulmer's XI	Londesborough.
Sat. 13th	,,		
Sat. 20th	,,	Colonel Brooksbank's XI	Londesborough.
Sat. 27th	,,		
Sat. 3rd	Sept.		
Sat. 10th	,,		
Sat. 17th	,,		
Sat. 24th	,,		

Londesborough Park C.C. membership card 1887.

90

eleven and I sincerly hope it will not be allowed to remain inert'. It needed a public meeting in March 1896 to 'consider the feasibility of forming a cricket club'. There was 'a unanimous desire' to do so 'but the great difficulty was to secure a field'. Several sites were suggested before 'a deputation was dispatched to Mr. Thirsk with a view to obtaining the terms he would let the Horse and Foal Showfield'. As often happened, reformation brought more vigorous growth. In 1896 T. Mather was engaged as the club professional. He was hardly a startling success, averaging 4 with the bat and taking 20 wickets at 5.4 each. It was sufficient to earn his reappointment in 1897, but he managed only 6 wickets and 14 runs in the season. He was not retained. F. G. Cains was the most successful amateur in the side, averaging 20 with the bat and taking 60 wickets at just over 3 each in 1896. J. Richardson was also a useful bowler. The fixture list in that season included Hammonds, the York Depot, Stamford Bridge, Everingham and Melbourne.

The following season they negotiated a fixture against the powerful Beverley side from which professionals would be barred, but did bring in match professionals for some of their other fixtures, including 'A. Liddall, the Beverley and Pickering old pro.'. Since no Liddall is known in connection with Beverley, this may be a misprint for A. Siddall.

Alan Siddall was one of the most successful professional cricketers to work in the East Riding. He was a farmer from Barmby Moor, but in the 1880's and 1890's he was virtually a full-time professional cricketer with a wide variety of clubs. Between 1887 and 1894 he formed a very effective partnership with W. Harbour at Londesborough Park. Harbour was employed to work in the joiner's shop on the estate and as the caretaker at the Hall, but his principal function was to act as the cricket coach to Lord Londesborough's family, a role he played for over twenty years. He was still taking wickets for Londesborough Park in 1911 and was regularly engaged by neighbouring clubs on a match basis. Siddall's career was much more varied. He was a talented all-rounder, who could command good match fees and was much in demand. In 1889 for example, he played for the Yorkshire Gentlemen, the North and East Ridings of Yorkshire XI, Lord Herries XI, York and Londesborough Park.

His value as a match professional can be illustrated by a series of games in 1897 when he was hired by the inexperienced Pocklington

Club. Against Driffield he scored 82* out of 112 and then took 3 wickets to help dismiss Driffield for 39. J. Richardson took the other 7. He then scored 63 out of 125 against Pocklington School, one of the few occasions when 'Town' beat 'Gown' and followed it up with 68 out of 106 against a Hull Thursday XI. In a rather unexpected fixture, he retired after scoring 100 for Melbourne against the Yorkshire Gentlemen. It is not surprising that when he turned out for Barmby in the Wilson-Todd Challenge Cup, Holme on Spalding Moor lodged a complaint on the grounds of alleged professionalism.

In some ways cricket in Pocklington seems to have been overshadowed by cricket at the school. The Pocklington Masters ran a side and the town clubs never seemed to develop firm roots. The lack of a permanent ground was probably part of the problem. The Horse and Foal Showfield does not inspire confidence and the club moved to a new ground in 1897. When the young club achieved its first success in 1897, winning the Wilson-Todd Cup by defeating North Cave in a thrilling match, they played the game on the school ground. The enthusiasm for cup cricket was again demonstrated when a brass band led the successful team from the school to their headquarters at the Waterloo Hotel. That success should have led to a period of consolidation, but the club disappeared at the turn of the century, leaving cricket in the town in the hands of Pocklington All Saints, playing on the West Green and the Wesleyan Guild. A different kind of sectarianism was in evidence in 1903 with the formation of the Pocklington Liberal C.C., who were strong enough to run a second eleven in 1905. They too played on the West Green. Pocklington Amateurs, Pocklington Wednesday and Saturday sides all paint a rather sad picture of dilution. It was 1909 before a Pocklington Club was started again, but it could not command a prominent place in East Riding cricket.

Alan Siddall played a full season with Beverley in 1895 and 1896, opening the bowling and batting at number four. The move to Beverley was probably the result of a tantalising episode in Londesborough Park's history when it was announced that it was 'impracticable' for the club 'to carry on' and they could not fulfil their fixtures. The nature of the problem is not known. A game against Driffield in 1894 was played 'on a very bumpy wicket' on which Londesborough was dismissed for 26, the Driffield pro., Storer, taking 8 wickets for 9 runs. There may have been a problem with the ground at Park Farm, particularly as by this period the Londesborough family tended to live at Blankney Hall in Lincolnshire, but there is no evidence that the Earl withdrew his patronage. For the same reason, a financial crisis, though the most likely explanation, seems difficult to understand. Whatever the cause of the problem, the players went their various ways, Siddall to Beverley and E. W. Usher to Driffield, where he topped the batting averages in 1895. Londesborough Park did play Pocklington School at the school in 1895, which preserved their continuity as a club. Whatever the difficulty was, it was resolved by the 1896 season, when J. Falkiner supported Harbour as the professional.

Lord Londesborough's death in 1900 tended to change the character of the club. Country house cricket was not as prominent. The 2nd Earl began to sell off the outlying areas of the estate but retained the Londesborough portion[6] which meant that the Cricket Club had the advantage of playing in a superb country house setting, whilst taking on many of the characteristics of a village club that could more than hold its own with the town sides in the Riding. In many ways it had the best of all worlds.

It certainly thrived in the early 20th Century. In 1903 the batting was opened by W. A. Usher and E. W. Usher. The latter was the mainstay of the batting for a number of years, regularly topping the averages with 68.24 in 1905 and 42.66 in 1906. Frank Mitchell made a handful of appearances in 1905, scoring 81* against Shiptonthorpe, but it was W. D. Featherby who was to become Usher's opening partner from 1906 when he averaged just over 20 from 12 innings. He replaced Harbour as the leading bowler in the club in 1908 and by 1910 he was scoring heavily (636 runs at 35.3 with a highest score of 137*) and taking 60 wickets at 4.53. He had been summoned to the Yorkshire nets in 1909 in the brusque way of the County, 'terms 10/- per day and 3rd class rail fare', but he was to have an unfortunate county career, playing against Derbyshire and Worcestershire without having the chance to bat in either match and taking 0 for 12. It is a county record that does not do justice to his ability.

The most talented cricketer from the Market Weighton area was Frank Mitchell, whose talents as a cricket and rugby player were obvious at St. Peter's, York, before he went on to Cambridge. He was the cousin of J. R. Mortimer, the Driffield Secretary and later the captain of the club, who invited him to play occasional matches for Driffield between 1891 and going up to Cambridge in 1894. His talent was quickly recognised by Lord Hawke, but even so, not many young Yorkshiremen have been in a position where they 'expressed a wish to the county authorities to play for Yorkshire against Middlesex' and have those wishes acceded to. He had a distinguished career with Yorkshire and played two tests for England in South Africa in 1899. He had toured that country with Lord Hawke, served there in the Boer War and settled there for some time. His career with Transvaal led to the captaincy of South Africa on their 1904 tour, when they were not given a test match, and the 1912 tour when he played in all three tests. His six caps for England at Rugby completed a distinguished sporting career.

Sources

[1]   J. T. Ward *East Yorkshire Landed Estates in the 19th Century* East Yorkshire Local History Society 1967 p. 17.

[2]   Hodgson p. 17.

[3]   Ibid p. 42.

[4]   J. Lonsdale *Yorkshire United?* an article in The White Rose, February 1986.

[5]   Holmes p. 170.

[6]   Ward p. 18.

CRICKET ON THE COAST

Cricket from Withernsea to Scarborough had an element that was missing from the rest of the Riding. The popularity of the Victorian seaside drew a steady stream of visitors by train to the coastal resorts of Hornsea, Bridlington, Filey and, stretching a geographical point, Hunmanby. The practice of whole towns taking the annual holiday at the same time, meant that many of the holiday-makers were known to each other and often contained the nucleus of a cricket team. Local teams were willing to play a Visitors' XI not least because such a match would bring a wealth of partisan support through the gate. In some ways cricket on the coast could be less exclusive than with the other clubs, but there was always the possibility that a gentleman cricketer would take up residence for the summer and strengthen the local side.

It is unlikely that the Bridlington Cricket Society of 1820 survived for very long and nothing is known of any other club. As elsewhere in the Riding, the crucial period is the 1840's, when there is a definite sense of a revived interest in the game. 'On Tuesday week, a match was played between two elevens, one belonging to Filey, the other to Hunmanby in a field near the latter place. The Hunmanby went in first, but could not stand against the bowling of their opponents, losing all their wickets in six overs and obtaining only 12 runs. The Filey men took the bat and having scored 143 for the loss of 8 wickets, their opponents gave up the match, owning themselves completely beaten'. Filey would seem to have been an experienced side, but it is possible that cricket had not been played in Hunmanby for some time before this September 1843 match. A Scarborough v Filey and Visitors XI is recorded in 1849.

The pattern is not dissimilar elsewhere. When Bridlington played Scarborough in 1852, it was seen as 'being quite a novel affair in Bridlington, the first match of the kind ever played here. It caused a good deal of excitement and several hundreds of people in the course of the day, visited the scene of the action'. Bridlington's performance, a six wicket victory, suggests that they had some experienced players. The club survived until at least 1855, but then 'it

95

dwindled away to nothingness, many of the players leaving the town'.

A new club, the Bridlington and Quay Cricket Club was formed in 1863 at the same time as clubs were started in Flamborough, Barmston and Sewerby. The sense that cricket was something of a novelty in the Bridlington area is seen in the advice given to the new club that should 'it become a strong one, we recommend an instructor should be hired to teach them for a short time, as there are only a few who know ought of this game in the locality'. Flamborough and Sewerby, who put out a joint side in 1864, were fortunate to be coached by an experienced York cricketer, who had moved there for the summer, but W. Perfect's coaching was wasted on Mr. Simpson, whose bowling 'though strong and tolerably straight, was not at all in accordance with the 10th rule'. This is likely to have been another round-arm bowler with his arm above the shoulder.

The key figure in Bridlington cricket in the 1860's was Robert Baker. He had played for the town against Scarborough in 1852. scoring 51, but didn't move from Hunmanby until 1863. He was the driving force behind the formation of the Bridlington and Quay Cricket Club that practised 'every evening in the new field situate near the rifle range'. The club used the Black Lion as their base. Baker, the two Crowe brothers from Flamborough and I. Bointon, a talented wicket-keeper, formed the nucleus of the side. Baker became the secretary and Marmaduke Prickett, a local J.P. and a leading figure in the town, became the President. Prickett was no mean cricketer, scoring 63 against Driffield in 1864. Guest players were invited to strengthen the side, 'ours being a young club' and Ralph Teal and (inevitably) Francis Matthews of Driffield were regulars in the early teams.

The coaching of two professionals, Piper in 1865 and J. W. Sagar in 1866-7, no doubt improved standards and it is a measure of the progress that was made that they beat Hunmanby by an innings and 35 runs. Hunmanby had not lost for two years and 'long odds had been laid on them', but 'Mr. Braby's slows puzzled the Hunmanby men greatly. They were either enticed to run in and miss and get stumped or the ball was skied'.

Baker had ambitions to establish a club that would rank with any in the Riding, but inevitably when they faced strong opposition the difference in experience and perhaps ability, was highlighted.

Playing against Terry and Crossland, 'a host in themselves' can only have been beneficial, but when Baker arranged the first two day game, in 1865, '22 of Burlington and District against 11 of York' (including Matthews!), it may have been 'red letter days in the annals of cricket at Burlington', but the gulf was all too apparent. The local side was strengthened by amateurs from Hull, Driffield, Hesslewood and Hunmanby, but was skittled out by George Freeman, Ferrand and Osborne. Only one player managed 10 and York won comfortably by an innings.

Perhaps Baker realised that he had been over ambitious. When Bridlington played a strong Scarborough side in 1867, he imported Ullathorne, Green, Cole and Brown to play alongside Sagar. At least two of these were professionals and all would receive travelling expenses. Such ambitions put a strain on the club's finances. They had the advantage of the holiday-makers in the season, but the admission charges of 6d for adults and 3d for children were far higher than most clubs charged for ordinary games. Nevertheless, on the surface, the club seemed to be thriving. The names of 25 playing members are known for 1866 and there was a juvenile section that played several games.

The importance of Baker to the club is seen in the 1866 averages, which include uniquely, a 'number of overs' column as the decimal part of the batting average.

Batting:	Inns	Runs	Av	No of overs
R. Baker	20	320	16	0
R. Crowe	20	260	13	0
J. Sagar	6	71	11	5
M. Prickett	9	61	6	7

Bowling:	Balls	Overs	Runs	Mdns	Wkts	Wides	N.B.
R. Baker	1617	269	431	80	82	26	2
J. Sager	754	125	147	54	46	1	6
R. Crowe	684	114	232	28	38	25	1

The professional's performance in bowling 125 overs for only 147 runs is a remarkable one.

When Baker left the town to become the Town Clerk of Scarborough in 1868, he was given a cane handled bat inscribed:

'Presented to Mr. Robert Baker by the Bridlington and
Quay Cricket Club for his valuable services as Secretary.
14th April 1868'.

He went on to have a distinguished career with Scarborough, where he was the secretary of the club from 1869 until his death in 1896. He once took 5 wickets in 5 balls against Malton and played three times for Yorkshire as an amateur between 1874 and 1875.

He was missed in Bridlington. A letter to the *Free Press* in 1869 produced a surprising debate. 'For the past two years, I have noticed with great regret the utter falling away of our Town and Quay Cricket Club and can not help thinking that something might be done to raise it as good an elevation as when Mr. Baker was amongst us. But it seems to have arrived at the pitch when four or five matches at the most constitute our cricketing season and even then the Bridlington Club had to be made up from other elevens in the neighbourhood'.

The following week there was a detailed reply written under a 'nom de plume', but obviously from a committee member. The writer paid tribute to Baker's work as secretary, but argued that he had been 'so keen to win that he introduced strangers'. That policy, together with 'other questionable expenditure', had placed the club in serious debt. He produced two sets of figures to show how the club had been forced to retrench over the last two seasons:-

In 1867:	Paid Sagar for bowling	£18.16s. 0d.
	Paid travelling expenses	£ 5.13s. 0d.
	Paid others (not of club) to play	£ 3. 7s. 0d.
In 1868:	(when no professional was employed):-	
	Paid travelling expenses	£ 2. 0s. 2½d.

The committee had tried to limit costs by arranging matches limited to club members. Ganton had agreed to play only bona fide members but had turned up with King, the ex-Scarborough pro., Fawcett, a pupil of Freeman's at Malton and Matthews of Snainton, 'perhaps the best bat of that neighbourhood'. It was unrealistic to face some opponents without strengthening the side. Malton, a club with 180 members, still brought in additional 'cracks', including 'one playing under the alias of Mr. Jones'. Bridlington had felt obliged to pay Drake and Ullathorne to play for them if they were not to be outmatched. The club's officers were continuing in office only to try to manage the debt and intended to resign at the end of the season. He ended his long and revealing letter by arguing that the club needed to change its ground to one near the Crown Inn. 'The young men of the Quay will not go up to the present remote place and those of the Town desire to spend their leisure nearer the attractions of the Quay'.

The threat of resignation was carried out and the club folded, but at the start of the 1870 season it was resolved that 'a new club be formed under new management' based on the Crown Inn at Quay Road. Subs were to be 5/-. They had a new President, Dr. Nelson, but kept the same name and several of the new committee, including Kirby and the Crowe brothers, had been prominent players in the old side. The transition seems to have been perfectly amicable. They purchased the equipment of the old club and instructed the secretary 'to arrange with Mr. Barugh respecting the field and to prepare the same for the opening match to be played on 2nd May'. A club formed in April and playing on a new ground in May is a further testimony to the standard of wickets at the time.

The 1870's is a confusing decade in Bridlington cricket and is not helped by the sparsity of reports in the Bridlington *Free Press*, which almost ignored cricket in the town. Most information is to be found in the papers of neighbouring towns. The Bridlington and Quay C.C. formed in 1870 moved on to a new ground 'near the gas works on Quay Road' in 1871, but were not pleased with it at first. They were strong enough to run a second eleven in 1872 and were said to have achieved 'many victories', few of which were reported locally. According to the *Driffield Times* they won 23 of their 31 games in 1873 and 'were rapidly acquiring prestige and with good management and mutual forbearance there is no reason why it should not become one of the first clubs in the East Riding'. Capt. Ledger topped the batting averages with 338 runs at 16.2, whilst R. J. Miller took 80 wickets at 5.0 a piece. Miller was the captain. His professional career was over by 1870, but like many slow bowlers, he was able to play for a long time. When he took 8 wickets against Driffield in 1886, it was reported that 'he still retains some of the talent that distinguished him in his professional career'. A decade earlier he had taken '5 wickets all clean bowled in one over, three in succession, thus becoming entitled to a new hat'. He was still playing for Bridlington in the 1890's.

The hints about good management and mutual forbearance point to the club's heavy debts. They tried to clear these by arranging a match against The Clown Cricketers, a group of talented professionals who put on entertainments rather than straight matches, but the club still had to admit in 1874 to being 'in a bad way'

99

and had to appeal to the local gentry and tradesmen for help. Their income from all sources was £108 and they actually had a balance of £9.4s.7d. on the 1875 season, but had accumulated debts of £35. Two galas arranged to raise funds were both rained off, plunging the club further into the red. The debts no doubt help to explain the absence of professionals in these years.

There was a further complication. Matches were played in 1872 and 1873 between Bridlington and Bridlington Quay. A similar match was played on the Town Ground in September 1875. It is possible that these were internal club games in much the same way that other clubs arranged 'Marrieds' v 'Singles', but it is a pointer to the internal divisions between the 'old' and 'new' towns that had been mentioned in the 1869 letter. No cricket was reported in Bridlington in 1877, but the following year a meeting was held at the Alexandra Tap 'to form a cricket club for Bridlington Quay'. They were playing 'on the Quay ground' in 1880 and encouraging visitors to join them for the summer season for a 2/6d subscription. In the same season 'Bridlington' were playing 'on the ground in Applegarth Lane, near to the Priory Church'.

The two clubs are not always easy to distinguish. As was common in Victorian times, leisured gentlemen joined and played for both clubs. In the early 1880's, Miller, Radford, Clarke, Hicks, the Rev. C. Corbett, Thompson and Capt. Ledger played regularly for both sides and 'visitors' could be added to the list. There was little difference between the fixtures and there is a suspicion that newspaper editors sometimes shortened Bridlington Quay and Visitors C.C. to Bridlington C.C. in their reports. Tentatively, it would seem that when Bridlington C.C. moved on to the 'new public recreation ground' in 1885 they began to be perceived as the town's premier club, but the Quay continued to have Bridlington's leading players in their teams and were ambitious enough to propose engaging a professional in 1903. Their President for much of these years was D. F. Burton of Cherry Burton. The Bridlington Priory Church Institute Club took over the Applegarth Lane ground and played in various divisions of the Hull Alliance League at a reasonable standard in the 1890's. They produced at least one professional, C. Miller, (possibly R. J. Miller's son) who joined Horwich in 1896.

The proliferation of clubs was not unique to Bridlington and could be mirrored in Driffield, but it undoubtedly lessened the impact of Bridlington on East Riding cricket in the 1880's when neither the Town nor the Quay were perceived as being as strong as Hunmanby Mitford.

There was an opportunity to combine forces in a District XI in 1888 and again in 1892, against two interesting touring sides. The Parsees, under the captaincy of P. D. Kanga, were the second Indian side to visit England. They were not particularly strong, but in Dr. E. M. Parvi they had a useful bowler who was the first Indian ever to perform the hat-trick. He found conditions in Bridlington to his liking and took 14 wickets in the match, which the Parsees won by 20 runs. This was followed by the first ever tour of England by a Dutch side. League cricket had been established in the Netherlands in 1891 and they could put out a very useful side. C. J. Posthuma, the captain, was 'well up to English first class standard'[1] and had been invited by W. G. Grace to play in his London County team. The tourists had the better of a drawn game.

In between these two games was what must have been the low point of Bridlington cricket when the club was dismissed for 4 by West Hull.

WEST HULL v BRIDLINGTON 1889

WEST HULL:

P. Frith	c Woodcock	b Taylor	3
J. P. Blackwell		b Southwell	5
C. P. Sharwood	c Cranswick	b Southwell	0
T. R. Smith	not out		29
A. J. Walkington		b Southwell	0
H. Rippon	lbw	b Southwell	0
J. Nutt	c Miller	b Burton	0
G. A. Tate		b Taylor	15
W. Wheatley		b Taylor	0
G. W. Tonge		b Miller	2
G. M. Shepherd	run out		4
	Extras		0
			58

BRIDLINGTON:

H. Cranswick		b Walkington	1
Hardwick	run out		0
J. Cranswick		b Blackwell	3
D. F. Burton	run out		0
J. J. Woodcock		b Walkington	0
H. Taylor		b Blackwell	0
T. L. Radford	not out		0
F. J. Brigham		b Blackwell	0
O. White		b Blackwell	0
(Southwell and Miller absent)			
		Extras	0
			4

At the turn of the century Bridlington had some talented players. The core of the side was a family of farmers and auctioneers, the Cranswicks, who on occasions turned out a complete cricket eleven from within their own ranks. Joe Cranswick was the Bridlington captain in 1899, whilst W. H. Cranswick, a Yorkshire Colt, J. Cranswick, A. Cranswick and H. S. Cranswick all played at times for the club and Hunmanby Mitford. The leading bowlers were Major Lowish and T. Woodhouse, who later on became the professional at Filey. The fixture list however, was distinctly unambitious. They retained matches against Scarborough 2nds, the two Driffield sides and Filey, but the rest of the games were against Hessle, the N. E. Railway Clerks, Hammonds Stores and various Hull church sides such as the Congos and Brunswick Wesleyans.

In 1900 they engaged J. Falkiner as their professional and groundsman. He was a seasoned pro. who had been around the clubs in the Riding for a number of years, but although he turned in some useful performances, he seems to have given up playing by 1905, when he only played one innings and did not have a bowling average, to concentrate on the ground. The club did begin to put together some more impressive performances, winning 13 of their 25 games in 1904 against better opposition that included Hull An XI, Leeds Police, Leeds Springfield, Wakefield and Rotherham teams, but the club was rent by internal divisions and had a massive debt for the time of £150. It was said to be 'in a hopeless state of insolvency' and to have 'allowed the pavilion, plant and ground to get into a seriously dilapidated state'.

The Cranswick family XI. H. Cranswick and J. Cranswick in the middle of the centre row.

It was reorganised in April 1905 under new management with Arthur Cranswick as secretary. 'There was not much of him, but what there was, was good.' Under his guidance the club was rebuilt, literally in one sense, since a new pavilion designed and erected by club members, was constructed in the south-east corner of the ground in 1908. He must have been largely responsible for persuading Yorkshire to stage a 2nd XI fixture against Cheshire on the ground in 1909. The amateur gentlemen of Cheshire were comprehensively beaten, but the two day fixture in August attracted 1000 holiday-makers and a £29 gate, which more than satisfied the Yorkshire committee, which rewarded the club with a match against Surrey 2nds in the following season and a game against Bridlington and District in 1912. Surrey so enjoyed their visit that they specifically requested that a future fixture should be played at Bridlington. When that game was played in 1913, a local bowler, George Bayes of Flamborough, who had moved to Scarborough via Bridlington, opened the bowling for the Yorkshire eleven. He had played for Bridlington as a 21 year old in the 1905 season and had made his County debut in 1910. His first class career had the misfortune to span the 1st World War, but he took 39 wickets for Yorkshire between 1910 and 1921. The gate receipts of £39 for the Surrey match in 1913 was the second highest for a county second eleven fixture that season and suggests that a pre-war August in Bridlington was an attractive venue for the county. This was not lost on the Yorkshire committee, which proposed matches against Lancashire 2nds in 1914 and Surrey in 1915, matches which, for different reasons were overtaken by events.

It seems unlikely that there had never been a cricket club in Hornsea before 1859, but if there had been one, it had faded from the collective memory. 'The Hornsea Club is quite an amateur one, having been formed only two months ago by the Rev. R. Nares (Curate), whose valuable exertions on behalf of it will long be remembered. This is the first club of the kind ever known in Hornsea and we have pleasure in stating that its first match was a successful one'. That match, which again underlines the importance of the clergy in encouraging cricket, had been played in front of 200 people at Wassand against Sigglesthorne, but no other match of this club is recorded.[2]

The railway came to Hornsea in 1864 and this may well have encouraged the formation of Hornsea C.C. in 1865, since it opened

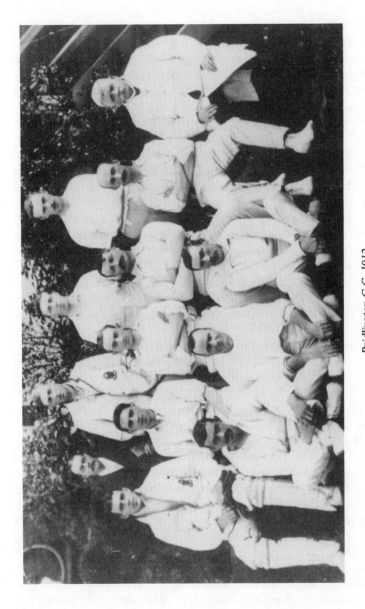

Bridlington C.C. 1912
Back: H. Hudson (scorer), J. Southwell, H.S. Cranswick, R. Railton. Middle: G.S. Blagborough, C. Middlebrough, W. Cooper (Capt), T. Crowe, C. Gane (umpire). Front: F. Bailey, J. Rollison (pro.), J. Allerston.

up the prospect of matches against the Hull clubs, most of which were only too pleased to accept a fixture on the coast. From its foundation Hornsea was ambitious to play against the well established town clubs rather than against neighbouring village sides, but since the resort was no bigger than a large village, with well under 2000 people, the only way in which it could compete was by bringing in guest players, often in surprising numbers and by hiring professionals on a match basis.

They were able to do so because they had the support of a wealthy patron, Joseph Armytage Wade, who became the President of the Club. In the early days, the description 'the Hornsea Club (Wade's)' was used more than once. He was a Hull timber merchant, a major landowner in Hornsea and an entrepreneur who was instrumental in bringing the railway to the town amid schemes to develop it as a resort. He did succeed in building a pier 'but Hornsea throughout showed a stubborn reluctance to accept any such conditioning programme' to be turned into a resort.[3] One of the noticeable differences between Hornsea cricket and that at Bridlington, Filey and even Withernsea, is the absence of Visitors' teams in the summer. Wade provided the club ground close to the station, between the railway line and Stream Dyke. R. J. Wade became the Secretary and Treasurer.

Occasionally the practice of relying heavily on guest players was resented. A match against Beverley in 1868 was 'ostensibly between two elevens of the clubs, but really between eleven of Beverley and seven picked men from Hull and the remainder from Hornsea'. Driffield pointedly printed the home clubs next to the names of one Hornsea XI to show that only three players were actually members of that club. Driffield made a similar complaint against Brandes-burton. 'Many of them are picked men. The Driffield club ought to be acquainted with the parties whom they have to meet and not to go blindfold to contest with a set of men picked from the different towns for the occasion'. There is a whiff of sour grapes. Both complaints had followed a heavy and unexpected defeat. It was unfair in yet another way. The Hornsea Club was based on Hull and Holderness rather than the town. The membership list for 1869 shows 90 members, 36 from Hull, 33 from Hornsea and the remainder from a very wide area.

In 1869, strengthened by Wright, the Hull pro., Ullathorne, Lee of Leeds and Twiss, the Hull keeper, Hornsea entertained the

Bridlington C.C. about 1914

Back: Taylor (umpire), J. Southwell, ?, C. V. Gane, H. Hudson (scorer). Middle: ?, W. Cooper, F. Allerston. Front: ?, J. Rollison (pro.), ?, F. Bailey, G. Middlebrough.

107

powerful Newark side and defeated them by 57 runs. It was their most significant achievement to date and the beginning of a most ambitious programme over the next few years.

By 1871 they had completed an adventurous programme of developing their ground, 'spending considerable sums on levelling it'. Interestingly they called on the expertise of Constable, the Hull professional who had been given specific responsibility for developing the Argyle Street wickets, to work alongside one of the members, A. Brittlebank, in supervising the work. 'The wicket was made firm by laying railway sleepers in the ground, bedded in ashes and then turfed over. A small pavilion was put up'.[4] It both underlines the close links that existed between Hornsea and the Hull clubs and is further evidence of the moves by Riding clubs to improve their wickets in the 1870's.

It may well be that the newly improved ground was the reason for inviting the United South of England Eleven to play a three day match against a District 22 at the end of August 1871. The decision to engage a professional for two afternoons a week, may also have been part of the preparations for that game. The club had been fortunate to have G. N. Ash join them, 'a magnificent bowler' according to Lilleywhite's Cricketers' Companion. The professionals who were brought into the local side, (Constable, McIntyre, Howitt of Middlesex and Pinder, the Yorkshire keeper), the travelling expenses and fees of the southern 'cracks', together with the expenses of putting on the game, add up to a considerable financial commitment. Realistically any expectations of a large gate depended on fine weather tempting large numbers from Hull on to the special trains negotiated with the railway company, so it is pleasing to find the club making a £10 profit on the match. The teams were entertained to breakfast at the Alexandra Hotel as the guests of J. A. Wade and it may well be that the considerable developments at Hornsea in these years owed much to his patronage.

The touring side was without W. G. Grace, but with G. F. Grace, Lilleywhite, Charlwood, Willsher, Pooley and Southerton, it was a formidable force, which made the local side's victory all the more satisfactory. The scores were 94 and 60 for the South of England and 92 and 63 for 10 for Hornsea. They were invited back in 1874, this time with W. G. Grace. Jackson, the Hull professional, caught and bowled him for 11 in the first innings and bowled him 'with a shooter' for 68 in the second. 'Mr. Grace was missed three times (and he might have had another chance or two)'. Hornsea was perhaps let off lightly. In 1876 Grace batted until tea on the third day to score 400* against a Grimsby 22. It was the highest individual score recorded at that time.

Hornsea had engaged their first full-time professional, James Briggs from Nottinghamshire, in 1872. They retained him for three seasons before he moved on to Morley. T. Milnes was the pro. in 1875, but for the following season the club made the extraordinary decision to appoint Briggs' son, the 13 year old John Briggs, as their professional. He made his debut for Lancashire three years later and was to have a distinguished first class career, taking 2221 wickets, including 118 test wickets, and scoring 14,000 runs. In an interview in 1894, he explained that 'the club did not want a full time professional, and they thought I might do, though I could only bowl eighteen yards. I was pretty straight, but knew nothing about making the ball turn'. It was asking a lot of a 13 year old boy and it is not surprising that he made little impression in 1876. Despite this he was retained the following year, before being replaced by an older man, Hodgkins, 'as Briggs has been by no means as attentive as he should have been'.[5]

Not everyone was pleased to visit Hornsea. The reporter, who was detailed to attend the club's Athletic Sports, an event many clubs used to raise funds, was loud in his complaint. 'To commit a person to half a day at a small watering place like Hornsea in rainy weather, is one of the worst punishments we could wish to inflict'. He was the exception. Throughout the 1870's Hornsea had, perhaps rather surprisingly in view of its size and geographical position, a flourishing club that played on equal terms with the larger market towns of the Riding and which had a reputation for welcoming the better players from other clubs into its ranks, which ensured a good standard of cricket. They had a professional each season at a time when many clubs, such as Bridlington and Driffield had to manage without. The first century, 124* by A. Massingham against Sutton in 1878, was an indication of a very successful decade for the club.

With the benefit of hindsight it is possible to see the 1870's as the pinnacle of Hornsea cricket before the 1st World War. The club began to struggle in the 1880's. The development of a strong tennis section and a new club in the town, Hornsea and East Holderness C.C. in 1875, provided strong competition for players. Hornsea C.C.

had always been seen as rather 'distant' from the town and there was a stated wish within the community to 'establish a thoroughly local club' which led in 1884 to the formation of Hornsea Town C.C.. Their first ground was in Southgate, but they soon moved on to one of J. A. Wade's fields close to the station and very near to Hornsea C.C.'s ground. The lack of interest within that club led to it folding in 1886.

The standard of cricket in the town over the next few years was disappointing. The Town Club lost the fixtures against the Riding sides and had to be content with playing against the Hull chapel sides, including the Central Hull Methodists' 2nd XI. J. Nattriss was the side's leading bowler during these years, taking 4 wickets in the first over against Hull St. Andrews in 1890 and 9 for 32 against Wilton St. Mary's in 1892, but the level of the opposition was a long way from the matches against Scarborough, Newark, Beverley and Hull of the past.

Ben Bolton, the Hull and Yorkshire County player, was a Hornsea man and played occasional games for the Town club in these years. He was one of the leading figures behind the formation in October 1893 of a new Hornsea C.C. by the amalgamation of the Hornsea Town Club with an occasional club, Hornsea Old Hall. Bolton became the captain. Although the fixture list was unambitious, the club had several successful seasons, employing W. G. Thompson as the professional in 1895. It was probably Bolton who drew 'Fred' Soulsby to the club and it is hardly surprising that the pair, who had been Hull's leading bowlers, proved an effective partnership, destroying many opposing sides. Sutton was dismissed for 5 in the opening match of 1896. Bolton had 6 for 0 against Hymers and Soulsby 7 for 10 against Hull Rovers, but despite these performances the club failed to put down firm roots and folded in 1899.

An attempt to form a Hornsea Zingari side got as far as gaining admission to the Hull 3rd Alliance league before folding, but over the next few years cricket was in the hands of a church side, St Nicholas and a chapel side, Hornsea United. It was a sorry story of frequent changes of ground, refusal to consider amalgamating and 'Hornsea ended the century with two clubs neither of which was strong enough to be considered representative of the town'.[6]

A new Hornsea C.C. was active in 1903 with several members of the Arksey family playing a leading role. Gradually a better fixture

110

Hornsea Thursday C.C. 1905
Back: H. Burnett, W. Whiting, T. Robinson, T. Huscroft, G. Scott. Middle: H. Miskin (?), G. Hind, J. Swales, T. Parker, Train,
T. Hunter. Front: Jackson, Bulmer, T. H. Arksey.

list was built up, but it was to be 1912 before Driffield for example, played against Hornsea. The cause of cricket in the town can not have been helped by the formation of the Hornsea Congregationalists in 1906, playing 'on the ground known as Wade's cricket ground' nor by the Hornsea Brotherhood C.C. which ran Saturday and Thursday sides from 1911, but closed down in October 1914. They can only have diluted the standard of cricket in the town. It was a rather sad end after such an auspicious beginning.

Hunmanby too had an influential patron. By the 1860's they played in the park adjoining the Hall and had taken the name Hunmanby Mitford after the lord of the manor. They had developed steadily after what had clearly been a shaky start in 1843. It may be that when they played Langtoft in 1861 'the sharp bowling of the Rev. C. Day and the slow bowling of Mr. C. Lamplough appeared to puzzle the eleven of Hunmanby very much', but they soon attracted some competent cricketers including 'Mr. Richardson of North Burton who, has succeeded in obtaining 15 runs off the bowling of England's XI'. When they lost to Bridlington in 1865 it was their first defeat for two years. They built up a fixture list that was nicely balanced between the village sides such as Langtoft, Ganton, Hackness, Muston and Wykeham and the club sides such as Scarborough 2nds, Bridlington and Filey Belle Vue. They had perhaps outstripped the Filey club by this time, as the latter only justified a game against Driffield 2nds in 1869 at the same time as Hunmanby was taking on a strong Scarborough side including King, the professional. Hunmanby had Drake, Ullathorne and Baker playing for them and tied the match at 92 runs each. By the 1880's they were recognised as 'one of the best clubs in the district', with regular fixtures against Malton, still the top club in the area, Hull, Pickering and Scarborough. The Yorkshire Gentlemen led by the Hon. M. B. Hawke played them in 1880.

They became one of the teams to beat. Occasionally this could lead to an excitable atmosphere as three matches against Driffield demonstrate. After the first, the Driffield club was advised 'either to make a charge for admission to future matches or obtain the assistance of a policeman to keep the noisy element more under control'. In 1881 the excitement spread on to the pitch. The Hunmanby side continually questioned the decisions of the Driffield umpire, and their own man, who was also playing in the match, refused to give out his fellow players on two occasions because 'I

112

couldn't see'. Matters reached a point where he and three other Hunmanby players 'refused to have anything to do with the second innings and left the ground'. After a third match, the Hunmanby captain wrote to the press, protesting at the way they had recorded the result as a win for Driffield. The following week a spectator wrote to express his surprise. 'It is true the Hunmanby umpire gave T. Scott run out when the winning hit was made, the batsman being well within the batting crease when the wicket was put down; it is also true that the Hunmanby umpire, captain and all the team walked off the field four minutes before the time fixed for drawing stumps, the score at that time being Hunmanby all out 80, Driffield 81 for 4'. No doubt it all added to the atmosphere of future matches.

Both Hunmanby from 1882 and Filey from 1891, made extensive use of professionals, often making use of Scarborough's and each other's on a match basis to strengthen their sides. Alf Smith put in some outstanding bowling performances for Hunmanby, taking 4 wickets in 4 balls in 1882 and performing two hat-tricks in the same season. 'He was presented with talent money'. He came second in the batting averages in 1886 with 27.2, only just behind W. H. Cranswick who had a top score of 152*. In the same season, the club's second pro., J. Falkiner bowled 180 overs for 233 runs, a remarkable degree of accuracy. It was not unusual for both Filey and Hunmanby to make regular use of three or four professionals in a season. It was not necessarily an expensive arrangement. In 1896, after the unexpected death of W. Thompson, Filey engaged Fred White of Cottingham, a 19 year old professional and groundsman with Wilson's Clerks in Hull, as their pro. for the season. He was given a twenty week contract at 25/- a week. In addition to his other duties, he had to make himself available 'to bowl at any member at all times of the week from 2.00 pm. except on match days'.

Filey, like most Victorian clubs, had its ups and downs, experiencing closure, reformations and changes of ground. A club was said to have been 'resuscitated' in Filey about 1870 and there was a major reorganisation in 1884. 'The club is now a *fait accompli*. A field has been secured and it will soon be in playing order. The finances of the club are in a flourishing condition and after all expenses have been paid, a considerable balance will remain in the Treasurer's hands. The club is now prepared to enrol members and arrange matches'.

Like all the other coastal resorts, Filey enjoyed mid-week fixtures against teams of visitors and touring sides, including Forfarshire in 1912, but their fixture list was not as strong as Hunmanby Mitford's. In July and August 1891 they played against Wykeham, Hunmanby, Scalby, Ganton, Bridlington, Driffield and Seamer, which is a good indication of their strength at that time. A two day match against Kirton-in-Lindsey in 1893 was unusual. One would like to know the background of Mr. Mavrogordato, who played for them in 1890 without any conspicuous success.

Filey had long had a close connection with the Holmfirth club and when they moved to their new ground on Muston Road in 1910, they arranged an ambitious opening match against the Huddersfield side, which included the pick of the Yorkshire County side. The Beverley pro., C. H. Mitchell, who came from the Huddersfield area, had gathered together a team that contained Rhodes, Hirst, Haigh, Bates and Broadbent. Filey had the services of Hunter, who was from Scarborough, Wilson, Newstead and Ringrose. Rain severely interrupted the game and discouraged the crowds, which made the day something of a financial disaster. Nor did the ground prove satisfactory. It had to be relaid in 1911 at considerable expense. It was perhaps an attempt to recoup some of these financial outlays that led the club to restage the match against Huddersfield. The two sides were essentially the same as the previous year, except that Filey included Bayes of Flamborough 'who upheld his reputation as the new fast bowler'. Unfortunately rain again spoilt the game, preventing any play before 3.00. Not surprisingly 'Hirst, Rhodes and Haigh proved very deadly with the ball' and Huddersfield easily won a rather disappointing match.

One aspect of cricket at the coast that remained unchanged throughout the Victorian period was highlighted by a Sheffield clergyman, the Rev. Alfred Haste, visiting Bridlington in 1904. 'I have much enjoyed my stay in your town. The sands are very fine, but I certainly think that the game of cricket should be prohibited on the sands, especially near the sea wall where the children and babies are in great numbers. Having seen the ball flying through the air to the danger of the lovers of the sand, constrains me to write to you'. It was one campaign that seemed doomed to failure.

Sources:

[1]   Bowen p. 148.

[2]   I am grateful to Mr. Jeremy Lonsdale for permission to draw on an unpublished essay *The Early Years of Hornsea Cricket 1859-1901* to supplement my own research.

[3]   K. A. Macmahon *The Beginnings of the East Yorkshire Railways* E.Y.L.H.S. p. 21.

[4]   Lonsdale.

[5]   Ibid. I have relied heavily on Lonsdale in this paragraph on Briggs.

[6]   Ibid.

THE LOCAL HERO

John Thomas Brown, a cricketer who was always much better known by his initials 'J. T.', was born in Driffield on 20th August 1869, where his father was the landlord of the Grapes in the main street. He learned his cricket playing with the Driffield Church Bible Class, a chance that might have been denied him if he had been born a few years earlier when he would have been unlikely to have had an opportunity to play for the more select Driffield Town Club. His subsequent progress to County and Test status is interesting for the light it sheds on the life of a young professional in the Victorian period.

In 1885, as a 16 year old, he is to be found opening the batting for the Church side and playing for the Rising Star. The following season he topped the batting averages for Marshall's club with 191 runs in 8 innings at 23.7. His highest score was 54. It is not immediately obvious what drew him to Yorkshire's attention, but he was one of four local colts who were invited to Sheffield to play against a county eleven. The other three were A. and H. J. Tinsley of Malton and W. A. Usher of Londesborough. Brown scored only one run but took 3 for 7 with his leg breaks. H. J. Tinsley had a few games for Yorkshire between 1890 and 1891, but there was no immediate follow-up to Brown's trial, nor did he set the world alight the following season, averaging only 10.6 with the bat, (176 runs in 19 innings with 43* as his top score) though he took 31 wickets at 5.4 for the Bible Class. That 43* however, was scored in 40 minutes of 'brilliant hitting'.

Despite his mediocre figures, his potential was recognised by Louis Hall, the opening bat for Yorkshire, who had seen him play for Driffield and recommended him to Perthshire as their professional for 1888. He went as a completely unknown 19 year old but ended the season as a firm favourite with a growing reputation. His benefit match against Forfarshire drew a large crowd and earned him £27.1s.6¼d. The ¼d no doubt reminded him that he was playing in Scotland! 'As a young pro. Brown, has to be congratulated on his success. He devoted himself with assiduous anxiety to his duties and shown fine form both as a bat and a fielder, while as a bowler he has come off very well for his first year'. He had 'endeared himself to many by his genial disposition'. He had every reason to feel pleased with himself, scoring 657 runs at an average of 31.6 and taking 92 wickets at under 6. It was hardly surprising that Perthshire retained his services for 1889, but it was felt by many who knew Brown, that the damp summer in Scotland accentuated the rheumatism from which he suffered all his life.

Yorkshire was no doubt kept informed of his development as a player. Hawke, the aristocratic captain of a team of hard bitten and, in some cases, hard drinking pros. had taken his time in assessing the situation, but now began to shape the side he wanted. Before the season there was no less than six colts' games to assess the strength of the youngsters in the county. Brown was called up and 'batted with the skill and coolness of a veteran' to score 72. He made his debut in July, scoring 59 against Leicestershire, but it was not a happy season for Yorkshire. They lost twelve matches and finished last but one in the table. Several county careers came to an end at the finish of the season, including those of Fred Lee and Irwin Grimshaw, whom the young J. T. had probably watched at Driffield in 1884. David Hunter and Brown were pencilled in as replacements, but J. T. found it difficult to make the breakthrough into county cricket to claim a regular place.

In 1890 and 1891 he had to be content with occasional games for Yorkshire and gaining professional experience with the clubs. He scored a fifty and took six wickets for Nelson and played against the Australians at Sheffield, but missed most of the 1890 season with severe rheumatism, though he played 23 innings for Driffield, only managing to score 334 runs at an average of 17. There were many critics who felt that he would not make the grade, but Lord Hawke and the Yorkshire committee clearly saw his underlying talent and were determined to bring him on slowly. 'We are what I call an ordinary team at present. We don't come across men like Peate, Bates, Peel and Ulyett every day. Though he has been criticised, I don't believe there is a sounder bat in Yorkshire than Brown at the present time. A man like him has to be made'.

At least Driffield benefited from Brown's Yorkshire experience. He played for them fairly often in 1892 and began to blossom as a thickset right-handed batsman, a ferocious cutter and hooker and a brilliant fielder at point or cover. He made several large scores and

J. T. Brown, Driffield, Yorkshire and England.

more interestingly brought several county colleagues to Driffield. C. J. Young's XI v Brown's XI became a regular fixture, with David Hunter appearing for Young and Ted Wainwright, who had broken into the County side in 1888, appearing for Brown in 1892. Young, incidentally, took 8 for 26.

1893 was probably the turning point in Brown's career. Both he and Young were professionals with Halifax, but early in the season Brown was in the county side against the Australians, played a match winning innings against Kent and topped the Yorkshire averages at the end of the season with over a thousand runs. He was still nominally the captain of the Driffield Club, but he can have played for them only rarely that season. He was also the captain of Driffield Rugby Club but was 'requested' by Hawke not to play rugby in the 1893-4 season. Such requests by Hawke were difficult to ignore.

At the end of the 1894 season, he was a rather surprising choice to tour Australia in Stoddart's side, for which he was to receive £300 plus his expenses. His exploits that winter were to make him a national hero. He scored four centuries, topped the averages and won the series with an innings that was straight out of *The Boys' Own Paper*. In March 1895 after four Tests, the series stood at two matches each. England needed 297 to win in their second innings and lost their first two wickets for 28. Brown then added 210 with Albert Ward, scoring 50 in 28 minutes and a century in 95 minutes, the fastest in test history. England won by 6 wickets and Brown returned to find himself fêted as the hero of the hour.

Driffield prepared to welcome 'Little Jack' home in style and to make him a suitable presentation, as did Hull and Halifax, which both made claims to him. In a sensitive gesture, the inevitable local committee limited the amount payable by public subscription to a maximum of 2/6d per person, which allowed no fewer than four hundred people in Driffield to subscribe to purchase a solid silver tea and coffee service inscribed:

> 'Presented to J. T. Brown by his friends and fellow cricketers in Driffield and the East Riding in commemoration of his achievements with Mr. Stoddart's team in Australia. May 17th 1895'.

A special match was arranged between a Driffield Eleven and an East Riding side consisting of Mitchell and Dunning (Beverley),

119

J. Cranswick (Bridlington), Cobb, Scott and Usher (Londesborough), Burstal and Bell (Hull), Breed (York), Hebblethwaite (Weaverthorpe) and Stead. Lord Londesborough agreed to make the presentation at the official lunch. Alas, the day was so wet that the match had to be abandoned and the marquee became so sodden that lunch could only be taken standing up in hats and coats.

Brown's career went from strength to strength. He formed, with John Tunnicliffe, 'the first great Yorkshire opening partnership',[1] scoring a record 378 against Sussex in 1897. Brown's 311 earned him a collection of £23.9s.9d. He spent the winter in South Africa as the pro. for the Cape Town Club and returned in 'better health than for some time'. This may well have been an important factor the following season when he and Tunnicliffe put on a world record 554 for the first wicket against Derbyshire. The feat was commemorated at the Scarborough Festival in 1900 when Yorkshire presented the two batsmen with silver cups inscribed:

Chesterfield 1898

J. Brown	not out	292
J. Tunnicliffe		243
Extras		19
		554

Brown had gone on to make 300 before breaking his wicket.

He went on to make 25 centuries for Yorkshire, play eight times for England and take 194 wickets. Hawke claimed that he had 'more of an eye for his figures than the rest of us' and it is clear that he could be a moody man. The official Yorkshire History recounts that 'he turned against alcohol, emptying all the beer in his house down the kitchen sink'.[2] The story loses some of its point if it is not realised that the house was his father's pub, The Full Measure.[3] That Brown was normally held in high esteem however, was shown beyond doubt by the public response to his benefit match against Lancashire in 1901. 40,000 people attended the game, contributing to a record benefit of £2282. It was proposed to send a special train from Driffield to Leeds, but even though the organisers guaranteed 600 travellers, the N.E.R. refused to put on a service, not the first time in the town's history that the railway company was held in low esteem.

J. T. Brown's last game for Yorkshire was in 1904 against Leicestershire when he was too ill to play on the third day. A top

London specialist diagnosed heart problems following rheumatic fever, no doubt made worse by his heavy smoking. Although it was reported in October that he was recovering, he died on 4th November 1904, aged 35.

Source:

1 Hodgson p. 67.
2 Ibid p. 67.
3 Article in *Driffield Times* based on the researches of D. Wells of Bainton.

VILLAGE CRICKET

The problem when writing about village cricket is that reports of matches are normally limited to the score-card and a few generalities. Fuller reports only occur when there was some bizarre incident such as the first match played by Wintringham, in which the village side 'refused either to continue the contest or relinquish the ball' after their best players were dismissed. The local paper sternly lectured them that 'men who can not gracefully accept victory or endure defeat would do well to abstain altogether'. Many present day cricketers, who remember waiting for the ball to be retrieved from the pond at Hutton Cranswick, will sympathise with the village cricketers of 1881, playing their first game on the Green, in which 'the ball found its way into the well and play had to be suspended while a ladder was procured and the leather recovered'. Duggleby turned up at Sledmere for their first ever cricket match with nine left-handed batsmen, only to be dismissed for 8 and adjourn for a very early tea at the Triton. When Withernsea played the Hull Mechanics' Institute in 1864 they gave away 85 extras in a total of 153, (65 byes, 10 wides and 10 leg byes). They were then bowled out for 45 and 31, which must make Withernsea one of the few teams ever to lose by an innings and one run to the extras!

Such incidents may raise a smile, but can create a false impression. In the 1850's and 1860's there was probably very little difference in the standard of cricket between the villages that had established sides and those in the market towns. After all, Pocklington, Howden, Driffield, Hedon, had populations of under 5000 and many of their best players, then as now, played for the village as well as the town club. There is nothing to suggest that those players dominated in the village side or were playing at a lower level. The situation was clearly different for those villages that were putting a side out for the first time, but the evidence would seem to suggest that most of them soon competed on equal terms.

Later on it was the improvement in the club wickets that was perhaps the most significant factor in the growing gulf between town and village cricket, but in the early days there is little to suggest that there was any marked difference. Indeed there is a case for saying that some of the villages may have played on better wickets than the town clubs. Cherry Burton, a village that played a lot of cricket in the 1860's, used the park of the squire, who, on more than one occasion, lavishly entertained the teams and provided iced champagne and sherry for the ladies at quite ordinary games. Middleton played their matches in 'the beautiful park' of Capt. Brocksbank, a ground that was regularly used for country house matches. Lord Hotham at Dalton Holme, staged two day games against the Yorkshire Gentlemen, probably the most prestigious of all the amateur clubs in the county, but allowed the village side the use of the ground. Lord Muncaster at Warter, Sir Clifford Constable at Burton Constable and several other of the gentry were prepared to open up their grounds to the village sides. It is difficult to accept that these villages were playing on wickets that were inferior to the Westwood in Beverley for example.

Ganton is perhaps the best example of the influence of a cricketing family 'at the Hall'. The three sons of Sir Thomas Legard 'were accustomed to bring down from Eton or Harrow several school fellows', who played cricket on 'the greensward, west of the back lane'. The family had the pitch relaid and engaged the Harrogate professional, Tom Burgess, as coach at the Hall. Over the next few years, the village produced two Yorkshire fast bowlers in G. P. (Shoey) Harrison, a shoemaker's apprentice in the village and Billy Ringrose, who was a carpenter there. His younger brother, Frank also turned professional, as did J. Cockerill with Liverpool and J. T. Clarkson with Bowling Old Lane. W. Fewster was a Yorkshire colt. All in a few years from a village of less than two hundred people.

Some villages could put out a very strong side. When Etton played two games against Bishopthorpe in 1858, (not the most obvious of fixtures), they found themselves up against five of the powerful York side, plus the seasoned professional Henry Dewse, presumably playing as an amateur. In the return game, after Bishopthorpe had scored 69, Etton crumbled before the bowling of Barrett of York, 'one of the best slow bowlers in Yorkshire', who took seven wickets. The first five Etton batsmen were out for ducks, but amid great excitement Earls (12), Bickers (27), Hallewell (15) saw Etton through to 69 and victory since there wasn't time to finish the second innings. Bickers was a Beverley player who had played

123

against the All England Eleven in 1849. Such a strong presence was by no means unique. Skidby could boast a county player in the 1880's and C. J. Young played in Fridaythorpe's first recorded match. Alan Siddall played for Huggate in 1885 and for Barmby in 1897.

There was always the danger in village cricket that one side could be completely outclassed if their opponents brought such 'cracks' with them. Siddall was presumably playing as an amateur for Warter in 1881, but both Storey and Usher were picked for representative matches and were noted local cricketers. Wetwang, one of the stronger village sides, can rarely have been so soundly thrashed.

WARTER

R. Smith		b Wilberfoss	3
J. H. Harper	thrown out		43
J. Storey		b Horsley	103
H. Ushger	c Horsley	b Ford	22
W. Rickell		b Horsley	14
F. G. Paley		b Wilberfoss	0
J. K. Rickell	c Larkin	b Horsley	4
A. Siddall	lbw	b Smith	5
W. H. Dobson	c Wilberfoss	b Horsley	30
J. Coxon	not out		25
T. Wilson			15
		Extras	21
			291

WETWANG

J. Smith		b Usher	0
W. Wilberfoss		b Usher	0
W. Lakin		b Usher	0
J. Wilson		b Usher	2
W. J. Parsons	c Wilson	b Siddall	2
H. Horsley	lbw	b Usher	2
J. W. Hopper	c Coxon	b Siddall	0
M. Piercey		b Usher	0
T. Ford		b Usher	0
R. Hopper		b Siddall	0
G. Beckett	not out		0
		Extras	1
			7

It was not unknown, then as now, for a village to introduce one or more 'cracks' into their team for important matches. When Weaverthorpe lost to Driffield by 17 runs in 1858, they put their defeat down to playing on a strange ground. The following season they negotiated a return match, but stipulated that the two elevens should be the same as in the first game in order to be a fair test of their strength. When the Driffield side arrived for the fixture they found that Weaverthorpe had brought in Cooper and Richardson, 'a first class amateur from the Langton Wold Club' and had even given him 'direction of the field during the day' i.e. made him their captain. Driffield took their defeat badly, especially when they learned that he and Cooper had never before played for Weaverthorpe.

The appendix at the back of the book lists the first recorded games of many villages. It needs to be treated with caution. It is certain that some village matches were played at an earlier date, but the local papers did not exist to record them. In other cases where no games are known before the 1880's it is likely that some villages had been playing for a period before reports found their way into the press. Even the case of Garton in 1860 where we are told specifically that it was 'the first cricket match ever played in the village' has to be treated with a degree of scepticism, though if it was not the first game it is difficult to see where the evidence is going to come from for an earlier match. The list should be seen as a base line which can be pushed further back into the Victorian period when, and if, new evidence emerges.

Nevertheless it does seem certain that for many communities this period was the start of village cricket. Etton formed a club in 1856, appointing John Whipp and Thomas Welburn as 'acting managers'. They attracted 30 members, including young men from Lockington, Cherry Burton and South Dalton, which would tend to suggest that those villages did not have clubs of their own in 1856 and to confirm that the Beverley clubs were inaccessible to many. Cherry Burton had a team in 1857, but it was the 1870's before the other two had any recorded matches.

In some cases it is possible to deduce that a village is putting out a side for the first time and that few of the players had any experience of the game. In July 1864 Nafferton played Garton. 'The Nafferton colts were unable to meet with a club with which they could compete with any chance of success and having challenged their betters, met

Beeford C.C., possibly playing against Frodingham C.C.

with a good thrashing which it is hoped may be beneficial'. Garton was the home of the Botterill's, two of the best Driffield batsmen of the time. Nafferton scored 13 in each of their two innings and lost by an innings and 72 runs. A week later, 'a match, not one of the most friendly' was played against Driffield 2nd XI, who 'selected two regular first team players, Mr. Burton and Mr. Botterill. The wickets were to have been pitched at 1.00 but owing to the Nafferton gentlemen demurring to two of the eleven selected to oppose them, play did not start till 2.00 p.m'. Nafferton may well have had good cause for their concern, as the score-card shows.

NAFFERTON

B. Sugden	not out		18
F. Owston		b Burton	9
W. Hoggard	c	b Wigmore	1
H. Piercey		b Burton	0
T. Crompton		b Burton	0
M. Owston	run out		4
J. Whittaker	c	b Wigmore	4
H. Goodwill		b Burton	1
J. Johnson		b Burton	0
A. Hind	run out		0
T. Whittaker	c	b Dunn	1
		Extras	8
		(sic!)	47

DRIFFIELD 2nd ELEVEN

J. Burton		b Sugden	108
Holtby		b Piercey	22
W. Botterill		b Sugden	89
Tonge		b Sugden	2
Wigmore		b Whittaker	4
R. Browne		b Whittaker	0
G. R. Jackson		b Whittaker	15
Brigham		b Whittaker	2
Dunn		b Whittaker	0
Dunning	lbw		0
Merkin	not out		7
		Extras	8
		(sic!)	255

Witherwick C.C. (or possibly Sproatley C.C.) in the 1890's. J. Nattriss of Hornsea C.C. is in the centre of the front row, holding the ball. Pipes were obviously compulsory to be at the front.

Such a score is without equal in any kind of local match before 1870 and is so far beyond the normal kind of scoring, both for a team and an individual, that it can only be regarded as an aberration and must add force to the argument that many of the Nafferton side were playing only their second game, though Sugden, Whittaker and the wicket-keeper(s) performed well. 'Mr. Burton's score of 108 has not been equalled on the Driffield ground and the members have, since the match, presented him with an excellent bat in commemoration of the fact'.

By the end of the 1860's a pattern seemed to emerge in which a club established in a village acted as a catalyst for the spread to neighbouring villages. Thus both Etton and Middleton had sides in 1856. Lund was playing in 1859, Garton, Kilnwick and Watton in 1860, Sledmere in 1861 and Wetwang in 1864. Geography normally dictated the pattern of fixtures, often with a close correlation to the catchment area of the local market town. Once established, the clubs, at least in the larger villages, were often on a very firm footing and less subject to the frequent winding-up and reformation that was typical of the towns. After playing their last match of the season in October 1863, a single wicket game because of the weather, Sledmere held their annual dinner at the Triton, where the secretary, T. Sharry, reported a membership of 70. Flamborough is perhaps one exception. They had a club in the 1860's which folded and the village was without a side for several years before the club was reformed in 1884.

The continuity in village cricket is also reflected in the team sheets in the appendix. Few people following East Riding cricket today will have difficulty recognising many familiar names in the village sides listed. Many family historians would probably have few problems in establishing four or five generations of one family playing cricket for the same village side.

It is hard today to realise how much the village cricket match was looked forward to as a means of reducing the numbing tedium of life in some Victorian villages. 'The monotony of Rudston was materially relieved last week by the announcement that a cricket match would be played in that village. (1868) A great many availed themselves of the opportunity of watching', of listening to the brass band and even taking tea with the teams at the Bosville Arms. Where the village didn't have a band of its own, one was often imported for the occasion, as when the Thixendale drum and fife band played at Bishop Wilton or the Huggate band was borrowed by Foxholes. The main attraction at the annual Cherry (Burton) Feast on 4th August each year was the village match, usually against Bishop Burton or Etton. Similarly the two day village feast at Holme-on-Spalding Moor in September each year, usually had a cricket match as a central part of the entertainment. A match between Sherburn and Weaverthorpe was arranged to coincide with the Flower Show at Wykeham.

A sense of occasion comes across in 1862 when Mr. Angas, a farmer at Neswick, arranged a match on one of his fields between an invitation eleven and a Driffield side. He erected a number of marquees to provide shade for 'a goodly number of the fair sex, who are generally supposed to be admirers of the noble game of cricket' and to house the lavish refreshments. The children of Bainton school were marched the mile down the lane to Neswick for the afternoon, watched the game, were treated to a generous tea and played sports on the field when the match was over, before returning home. It is difficult not to see such an afternoon as 'special' for those taking part. Cricket at North Frodingham, 'a dull dispirited village' and Wetwang, 'a besotted village, its inhabitants hateful and hating one another' must have done something to bring the community together.[1] It may well be one reason why the village clergy were so keen to promote a cricket team.

One aspect of village cricket that did separate it from town cricket in the 1860's and 1870's was that it was much more egalitarian. There was likely to be a much greater cross-section of society in the village teams than was evident in the restricted membership of the town clubs. Many sides included the local vicar and his curate. It was one of the few social occasions when the farmer and the village labourer met on near equal terms and several villages included the local aristocracy in their elevens. No doubt there was a sense of deference and a degree of forelock tugging when W. H. St. Quintin played for Scampston but D. W. Legard and Sir F. D. Legard batting four and five for Ganton against Sherburn, doesn't suggest too high an estimation of their batting prowess. Given the quality of cricketers turned out by that village it may have been a realistic assessment. Hotham and Birdsall were sides that regularly included gentry and, in general terms, it was not unusual for villages that contained 'a big house' to occasionally include a member of the family in the team. Indeed where the squires were cricketing

Ellerby C.C. 1912

enthusiasts, as the Burtons at Cherry Burton clearly were, the distinction between village cricket and country house cricket becomes blurred. In 1894 the village side tackled Filey and District, who turned up with seven professionals including one of the all time greats of Yorkshire cricket, Ted Peate, the slow left-arm Test bowler who was regarded by David Hunter, the Yorkshire keeper, as 'the finest left-arm slow bowler I ever saw'.[2] It should perhaps be remembered that Hunter also kept to Wilfred Rhodes. Peate was sacked from the Yorkshire side in 1887 by Lord Hawke because of his 'rapid decline', but this had less to do with his ability than his fondness for the booze. He may have been well past his best at Cherry Burton in 1894, but must still have proved a formidable opponent. Whatmough and Shaw from Scarborough, Falkiner and Smith from Filey, Thompson and Waller from Hunmanby, were the other six professionals and one wonders why it was felt necessary to assemble (and pay) such a strong side. Cherry Burton borrowed Charlie Mitchell, the Beverley pro. for the day and had the services of the Hon. C. Lambton, one of the Yorkshire Gentlemen Club, who was presumably a guest at the hall. Under the circumstances the village side did well to score 80 in reply to Filey's 140. The following week Lambton brought a side from the Yorkshire Gentlemen to play the village, this time strengthened by J. Shaw as the professional. Since the Yorkshire Gentlemen were still, in the 1890's, among the more prominent of the Yorkshire clubs, the fixture says much about D. F. Burton's standing and the quality of the wicket. His son, D. C. F. Burton was to captain Yorkshire after the 1st World War. In the next few weeks Cherry Burton played their matches against neighbouring villages with much the same team, minus the pros. that had played against the Filey and Lambton elevens.

The nature of life in the Victorian villages is reflected in several of the scratch sides that came together. Few farms today could put out a side to challenge a neighbouring village as Low Caythorpe farm did to Boynton in 1881. The staff of Sledmere House met those of Birdsall House in 1862. The Holderness Hunt stablemen and the East Riding Farmers played a few matches every season and there was a clerical side in 1872 that looked decidedly useful.

Given the number of villages playing cricket, it is obviously impossible to generalise about standards or to comment in any meaningful way about performances. One can applaud the honesty of the Cranswick captain, Rayner, who reported at the club's annual supper, that 'they were bad fielders, but they had one of the worst fields to play on (on the green) and when they were on a good ground they were at a disadvantage'. At Muston in 1874 'the wicket was bad and the grass being long, made runs very difficult to get'. If a village was not lucky enough to play on the better pitches provided by a cricketing squire, a growing gulf was likely to develop between the wickets played on by the village sides and those enjoyed by the town clubs. Many of the latter were employing professionals who often doubled as the groundsman. Most village grounds were quite small, which discouraged slow bowling and perhaps encouraged uncomplicated batting. Many of the best cricketers of the area continued, then as now, to play both for the town and the village, but from about 1880 onwards, judged simply on the score-cards, there is a distinction to be made between the standard of village cricket and that of the more sophisticated town clubs. If anything, this distinction seems to widen after 1900 when the length of time allocated to matches seems to shorten and single innings games become the norm, though examples of village teams trying, usually unsuccessfully, to play two innings matches in an afternoon may be found throughout the period.

What was clearly undiminished by 1914 was the popularity of village cricket in the East Riding. It had a vitality that was not always present in the senior cricket scene. The accounts of North Burton C.C. for 1908 reveal a cross-section of village life. Fourteen adult members of the village club paid 2/- each in subs, six boys paid 1/- and the vicar, the Rev. G. E. Park for some reason paid 2/6d. His wife, who bought the score-book for that season for 1/-, was also a member. She may have been the scorer, which must have been unusual for a vicar's wife of the period, The Treasurer spent 4/-on a cricket ball and 7/6d on a bat which was bound at a cost of 2d. The club's other bat cost 12/6d. The accounts proudly end 'In bank 9/6d'.[3]

The Parish magazines of the period give vivid cameos of the part played by cricket in village life. In 1900 Lockington and Aike played six 'foreign' matches, winning five. The rector captained the side and topped the averages. When Burton Agnes played Harpham, tea for both sides was provided by the Rector. Middleton had an excellent meat tea at the Robin Hood to follow their game. The sense of pride and achievement is only too evident in the announcement to the parish that 'after many years Bishop Burton has at last beaten Cherry Burton at cricket; a victory all the more creditable to Bishop Burton because the side was made up exclusively of natives of the parish'. Modern cricketers will not be surprised to learn that that Bishop team in 1900 consisted of 6 Ducks and a Swan.

Sources

1. Woodcock *Piety Among the Peasantry. Sketches of Primitive Methodism in the Yorkshire Wolds* 1889. p. 145 and 127.

2. Hodgson p. 44.

3. Information supplied by Mr. G. Beswick.

Langtoft C.C. complete with club caps about 1913.

A GOLDEN AGE?

'The Golden Age of cricket is usually regarded as stretching from 1890 until the outbreak of the Great War in 1914, during which years the game was just one manifestation of a seemingly endless Edwardian summer when the world was at peace, the sun never set, wealthy benefactors abounded, civilisation advanced and all humanity knew that things could only get better. It was the time of ..... the striped blazer, the boater, the parasol, an era of good manners and genteel courtesy..'[1]

Perhaps! Some historians might however, look at the period through less tinted glasses.

There was always a strong element of country house cricket in the Riding, large houses where like-minded friends and acquaintances could come together courtesy of a generous host, enjoy each other's company and play cricket matches that were not taken too seriously and where the overriding concern was not the result. Indeed to be seen to be striving too hard for victory might mean that future invitations were not readily forthcoming. Touring gentlemen, such as the I Zingari, who were defined in 1877 as 'a race of ubiquitous cricketers, who commence play before the mayfly is up and continue until the first pheasant is down' would have found many agreeable venues locally.[2] One such might have been at Ganton where Sir Charles Legard's Fox-hunting XI, with T. Burgess as the professional to prepare the wicket and do the bulk of the afternoon's bowling, played against the 16th Queen's Lancers. Another was at Everingham Park, where 'members of his Lordship's family and visitors' played matches, with C. Arnold hired to give some solidity if necessary. Mr. Sykes at Brantinghamthorpe Dale invited them over to play a match as part of the entertainment for a distinguished party of visitors, including the Earl of Rosebery and Lord Herries. Acey's band was in attendance as part of the entertainment. On that occasion the Everingham party contained no fewer than four Honourable cricketing members of the Maxwell family.

It could no doubt be said of any one of these venues, as it was of Tranby Park, 'that a more lovely spot for a game of cricket can not be conceived'. House and club cricket sometimes merged. Both Beverley and Driffield had regular fixtures against Tranby, who were said to be 'the pick of the Hull cricketers'.

Occasionally a local town club, with the suitable addition of some gentlemen and clergymen from the neighbourhood, was invited to play at the Hall. In September 1868 a considerable party from Driffield travelled by train to Brough, where they were met in person by Christopher Sykes, who made a short welcoming speech before guiding them into 'carriages of various kinds' for the journey to Brantinghamthorpe Dale. Tents and marquees had been erected around the pitch, which was in a natural ampitheatre. Luncheon was provided in the Hall for the Driffield party, followed by speeches and toasts. The pleasure grounds, shrubberies and gardens were open to inspection in the afternoon for those who wandered away from the cricket, whilst two bands entertained the spectators. After a lavish tea, the party was returned to Brough station. W. Jackson, the newspaper editor who had accompanied the party, was almost beside himself with admiration of what he had seen and the way he had been received. If the hospitality seems a little excessive for a side from Driffield, it should be remembered that 1868 was an election year, that Sykes was the Conservative candidate and that Driffield was split down the middle between the two parties. As Jackson expressed it, 'if Mr. Sykes be politically conservative, he is domestically and socially an out and out liberal'. Three weeks later when Mr. Sykes XI played Lord Londesborough's XI, F. C. Matthews had secured an invitation to play in Sykes' side.

Such cricket was essentially amateur in the sense that the competitive element was deliberately held in check. Club cricket, by its very nature, had a much sharper edge, but in the early days the wickets were such that scores were low, few batsmen could dominate and most matches came quite naturally to a satisfactory conclusion, even if it was on the basis of the first innings. The improvement in the 1880's and 1890's saw a shift in the balance and the potential for the batting side to dominate some matches. At this point it is possible to discern tensions coming to the fore. In effect it became necessary for the clubs to decide the degree of competitiveness that was desirable and acceptable in a match. It is probable that this was more an intuitive decision than a conscious one.

The laws did not help. Declarations were allowed for the first time in 1889. Driffield Marshall's Club playing against South Myton, 'decided to adopt the new rule and close their innings at 100 for 6'. It has never been difficult to get out in cricket and sides that wished to bring their innings to an end could easily find ways to do so before 1889. They did not always see any reason for doing it. In 1884 Hull batted right through their match against Pudsey. South Holderness scored 309 without reply against Hull 2nds in 1888. When Bridlington played Hunmanby in 1886, they scored 351 for 7, W. H. Cranswick scoring 152*, 'the visitors keeping possession of the wicket all p.m'. They repeated the performance later in the month, scoring 228 against Mr. Harland's XI and again in 1889 when they batted all the match to score 309 for 9, J. Cranswick scoring 101.

These were clearly extreme cases, but it was commonplace to find the side that won the toss choosing to bat and occupying the crease to a point where they themselves had little chance of victory. The matches seem to have been played at a very leisurely pace, with batsmen playing very cautiously and showing no real sense of purpose within the context of the game. It was pleasant if the game was won, but the result was of very little significance.

This attitude, taken to its extreme, was voiced by a Hull Zingari cricketer in 1902:

'You don't go down with the all-absorbing idea of winning by hook or by crook and pondering ways and means to accomplish the object. Whether you won or lost was not of the slightest consequence. It didn't matter whether you made a duck or a century, whether you took all ten wickets or none at all or if you muffed half a dozen catches or captured all ten men. It was perfectly immaterial. What you were wanted for, was not so much to distinguish yourself at cricket, as to contribute to a spectacle. Practically, the cricket match formed an excuse for a garden party, only it wasn't in a garden'.

It is perfectly possible to defend this approach to the game, particularly in the case of private clubs which arranged fixtures by mutual agreement for the benefit of their own members, though it has to be said that even in 1902, it was an attitude of mind that didn't fit easily into the Yorkshire and Lancashire way of looking at cricket. It becomes a much more difficult approach to defend when the clubs involved needed the revenues of paying spectators.

There was a good deal of contemporary criticism of the cricket being played. 'Another draw', lamented the *Hull Daily Mail* 'something wrong somewhere'. There were constant complaints about the lack of punctuality. It was 3.25 before the first ball was bowled when Zingari played Ferriby. The habit of batting on after a victory had been achieved seems equally open to criticism to modern eyes, but it did at least have the virtue of providing entertainment for the paying spectators, although it is doubtful if that was the motive. 'With nothing at stake the players have an excuse and a tendency to become apathetic and listless'.

One answer was to accept competitiveness into the game by organising league and cup competitions. League cricket began in Birmingham in the 1880's and rapidly spread in to the industrial areas of the north. The origins of League cricket in Hull can be traced back to the Hull and District Cricket Union in 1890, which was running organised leagues, certainly by 1893. These evolved into six Alliances (or Leagues), mainly, but not entirely, confined to Hull junior clubs and chapel sides. They made attempts to provide neutral umpires and to encourage prompt starts by fining clubs 1/-for every 10 minutes of delay. The Edwin Davis & Co. (a Hull store) Thursday Cricket League functioned in 1894, a mixture of works and church sides. The Leagues were extremely popular and were extensively reported in the local press, which began to distinguish between 'Ordinary' matches and 'League' matches. The leagues were anathema to the major clubs in Hull and the Riding, which turned their backs on any form of competition. As late as 1903 there was said to be 'a rooted antipathy at Anlaby Road to anything in the nature of competition'.

The attitude is the more surprising in view of the enthusiasm with which knock-out cup cricket was accepted even by the Hull Club. The Hull Town Challenge Cup became a major trophy when it was instituted in 1885, quickly becoming known as the Alderman Leake Cup after the President of the Hull Club. The Hull 2nd XI won it in 1885 defeating South Myton, but it may be significant that over the next two years the Cup was won by Riding clubs, Beverley United defeating Hull 2nds in 1886 and Marshall's Club defeating North Ferriby in 1887. Cup cricket undoubtedly captured the imagination of the public. The enthusiasm in Beverley after the 1886 victory has been described above, but it was to be echoed in Driffield the following year. There had been discussion about entering a joint Driffield United side in the cup, but when Marshall's won it on their own, they were met at the station as they returned by the 10.00 train and escorted down Middle Street by the band of the Rifle Volunteers.

There were other cup competitions, including the H. S. King Challenge Cup and a very ambitious North and East Ridings Challenge Cup in 1890, organised on a regional basis with three preliminary area competitions leading to a final.

By 1900 the position of the Hull Cricket Club with regard to competitive cricket was becoming untenable. The cricket correspondent of the *Hull Daily Mail*, 'The Major', ran a vigorous campaign to urge change. 'Cricket is fast losing even the little hold it once possessed on the Hull public and unless a combination is formed to put more life into the game, its prospects are anything but rosy' (1900). The club could have withstood this pressure easily enough, but the economic pressures were of much greater significance. There had been a considerable investment in the Circle, they had two professionals and the groundstaff to pay and depended on drawing considerable gates to avoid bankruptcy. The cricket season was much more restricted by soccer and rugby league than in the past. It did not begin until after they had finished in May and ended on 31st August when those sports began their season.

The harsh reality was that gates were falling through 'slow play and drawn games'. The antidote to bankruptcy it was argued, was league cricket on the lines of the Lancashire leagues. The crowds of 4000 to 6000 that had attended Hull's games in the past, had been drawn to see exciting cricketers such as A. P. Charlesworth, unusually for a pro. of the time, virtually a non-bowler. He was however a hard-hitting batsman who had brought in the crowds to pay their 3d at the gate. In contrast the Major had recently counted the attendance at a Hull v Rotherham match. It was, he declared, 43 adults, 4 boys, a loving couple, a handsome cabby, a dog and three hacks from the local press. 'Ordinary matches are all very well in theory, but in practice they are like plum pudding without plums ... eatable but not toothsome. League and cup-tie games have their disadvantages, but anyhow they have flavour and they do infuse a degree of enthusiasm and life into the players... more than can be said of the harmless Ordinary'. Many of the West Riding sides that Hull played against, had had a league competition, the West Riding League, until 1899, but 'from what I know of the management of the club, I can hardly bring myself to believe that they will take steps to cater for the democracy. They have always looked askance at anything approaching innovation'.

When the change came in 1903, it had all the signs of being hastily

Hull C.C. 1904

Back: C. Jordan (scorer), H. H. Marriott, W. Ringrose (pro.), F. Soulsby (pro.) W. Yiend, E. E. Sharp (secretary).
Middle: F. Asquith, H. Ostler, B. Bolton (Capt.), A. Waller, S. Robson.
Front: H. Rudston, B. Lawrence, G. Braithwaite.

brought in by the Yorkshire Cricket Council, a body that had been anti-league itself in 1900. Hull joined the Cricket Council Championship; York and Scarborough did not, so that fixtures against those clubs in 1903 were 'ordinary', a term that soon began to have overtones of secondary. Both joined the championship in 1904 when it seemed to be organised on a much firmer footing. By 1908, thirty clubs were members mainly from the West Riding, the exceptions being Hull, Scarborough and York. Hull played 18 Council matches a season, the championship being decided on a percentage basis as no club played all the other members.

There can be little doubt that the cricket changed. It can best be illustrated by a game against Castleford in 1904. The visitors scored 133 in 2¾ hours, leaving Hull 80 minutes to get the runs. They chased the win, the incoming batsmen running to the wicket to the encouragement of the crowd and won with two minutes to spare. It is impossible to believe that they would have tried to win such a match before the championship. It became much more common for Hull to put the opposition in and go for the runs. One trivial incident is perhaps symbolic of the changed attitude. The practice of the club was to give 10/6d talent money for 50 runs or 6 wickets, a guinea for 100. In 1910 with the professional, Rudston 91*, the captain declared to give enough time to win the match. It is hard to believe that that would have happened a decade earlier. It ought perhaps to be said that he met Rudston on the pavilion steps with the extra half-guinea out of his own pocket.

Although championship cricket, with the prospect of exciting finishes, did catch the public interest, crowds rarely reached the level of the old Argyle St. ground. The 3000 gate against Dewsbury in 1908 was seen as noteworthy, but the times were changing. The instant excitement of soccer and rugby league conditioned people to expect a different kind of entertainment. There were more leisure activities to compete with cricket. The popularity of cycling was seen by contemporaries as one reason for the decline. Hull C.C. was not the only club to suffer from a fall in interest in these years; Albert United, the Congos, the Church Institute, South Myton and East Hull had all folded by 1913.

The crisis for the premier club came in 1911. Only six of the previous thirteen years had shown a profit, and the Directors, who, after all, were responsible to the shareholders of the company, proposed to wind it up and negotiate a take over of the assets by Hull

142

City, the main one being the ground itself. The effect would have been to remove the top stratum of local cricket from the Riding, at least until a new club on a new ground could be established. It would have damaged the relationship with the County Club for the forseeable future and made the continuance of County cricket in Hull very unlikely. Not surprisingly, there was a public reaction. A group of shareholders led by Alderman F. Larard accused the Board of 'a want of enterprise in carrying on the concerns of the club'. They succeeded in setting up a committee 'to formulate a scheme for carrying on the club' and set out to raise the £2000 they believed to be necessary. They gained control. Larard became President, whilst J. Dunkerley, Beverley's benefactor, became prominent in the new regime. The *Hull Daily Mail*, in an article that caused some controversy, called for a more democratic approach to the running of the club and a more welcoming attitude to cricketers from the junior sides.

Hull survived, but faced a lean period. They could afford only one professional, Fred Halliday, a slow left-arm bowler, in 1911 and had a very young inexperienced team. They added Wrightson from Goole in 1912 and secured the services of Ben Emmett, an experienced wicket-keeper from Harrogate and 'a paid man for the last 12 years'. It is not clear whether Hull paid him. The team was a completely amateur one in 1913 and 1914, for the first time since 1865, but was fortunate to persuade their former professional and Yorkshire County player, Horace Rudston, to return to them as an amateur. He held the batting together in these years, in much he same way that another former player, G. Walker, who returned from a lengthy trial with Worcestershire, led a very thin bowling attack. The club owed much in these difficult years to the captain, G. Braithwaite, who seems to have led a very young side sympathetically.

Off the field, a more spirited approach by the new committee staved off the immediate crisis. Life membership offered for £10, season tickets to the pavilion enclosure for 10/6d. which included admission to the county match, afternoon teas served in the pavilion, may not have attracted many new working-class members through the gate, but it was enough to survive. The fire in April 1914 that destroyed Hull City's football stand and the cricket score board must have seemed another blow, but was soon to be surpassed by a greater conflagration that put it into perspective.

The Riding Clubs were not under the same pressure to adopt league cricket. Their financial problems were of a different magnitude, so that clubs such as Driffield were never as dependant as Hull C.C. on the gate receipts. When there was a difficulty, a special event such as Driffield Ladies v Hull Ladies, both sides bowling round-arm, in 1909 or Hull Gymnastic v Miss M. Staveley's XI, a serious game which produced over 300 runs, in 1901, was usually sufficient to raise the necessary funds. Driffield continued to play 'ordinary' matches in the way it had always done, though a single innings match played on the Saturday afternoon became the norm. Malton was reluctant to make this change, cancelling the matches arranged for 1892 'on the grounds that they do not play half-day matches'. The cricket was uncritically reported in the local press, which usually confined coverage of the matches to printing the score-card.

Driffield had some able cricketers in these years. Ernie Young turned professional in 1903 when he was engaged by Aberdeenshire. The captain from 1904 was James Mortimer, who returned to the club after serving in the Boer War. Given the link between Mortimer and Frank Mitchell, it may not be entirely coincidental that Driffield had a South African professional, T. W. Gill, in 1905, possibly the first overseas professional to play in the Riding, or that C. P. Carter, who toured England with the South African side in 1912, played for Driffield throughout the 1905 season. A spectator at the Driffield v Filey match in 1905 would have had the opportunity of watching two future county fast bowlers in opposition. George Bayes who was the match professional for Filey; C. P. Whiting, who seems to have reached maturity and to have bowled extremely quickly just before the 1st World War, was the young Driffield fast bowler. He put in some excellent performances, taking 9 wickets to bowl out Malton for 44 in 1914, the same year that he got in to the County side, taking 5 for 46, all bowled, against Essex. The first class careers of Bayes (1910-1921) and Whiting (1914-1920) straddled the war and must have been seriously damaged by it. C. P. Whiting took 15 wickets for 416 runs for Yorkshire. J. W. Teal, the professional from 1909 to 1914, was predominantly a batsman who scored 1000 runs in 1910 and a double century (200*) against Willerby in 1913.

There was no shortage of able cricketers. There were some close games. Driffield won 11 of their 19 matches in 1913, but it was cricket of a different age, a more leisurely age that had a greater certainty and self-confidence. Major Mortimer captained the side from first slip, the professional did his best to tie up one of the bowling ends and the gentlemen scored their runs and played their part. In 1909 a team of Oxford Tourists was bowled out for 71. Driffield, having reached the target, batted on to make 252 for 6. It can hardly have been exciting cricket. The local paper printed the scores without comment, but then the match was being played for the benefit of club members and was not seen as having any great relevance to a wider community outside the club. The pressures that were apparent in Hull were simply not an issue in the Riding before 1914.

The last match to be played in Driffield in 1914 was for J. W. Teal's benefit on 22nd August against Bridlington. It is a fitting end to an era.

BRIDLINGTON:

J. Rollison	c Hall	b Atkinson	17
J. Allerston	c Whiting	b Hall	7
J. Edmondson	not out		65
E. Maw	not out		43
		Extras	30
			2 for 162

DRIFFIELD:

M. Atkinson	retired hurt		34
T. Brown		b Blakesborough	20
C. P. Whiting	c Rollison	b Allerston	52
W. S. Hewson		b Allerston	2
P. H. Hall	not out	not out	23
Trooper Vernon		b Maw	10
		Extras	7
			4 for 148

The memorial to Lt-Col. J. Mortimer and the other club members who died in the war, is to be found in the wall next to the entrance to the Driffield ground. If Trooper Vernon came back in 1918, it was to a very different age.

Sources:

[1]   Hodgson p. 41
[2]   Box p. 466.

APPENDIX ONE
EAST RIDING CLUB PROFESSIONALS 1853-1914

HULL C.C.

1853-1857	A. Crossland	1889-1890	C. Oates
1859	A. Crossland	1891	H. Greenwood
1865-1867	A. Crossland	1892-1893	S. Malthouse, J. Dennison
1868	Job Greenwood,	1894-1895	A. P. Charlesworth
	Clayton	1896-1899	A. P. Charlesworth,
1869	J. Wright		P. 'Fred' Soulsby
1870	J. Burman	1900	P. Soulsby
1871	M. McIntyre,	1901	Ward
	A. Constable	1902	W. Ringrose
1872	G. Seaton,	1903-1904	W. Ringrose, P. Soulsby
	A. Constable	1905	W. Ringrose, H. Rudstone,
1873	Pocock		Grimshaw
1874-1880	L. Jackson	1906	H. Hinchcliffe, H. Rudstone
1881-1884	L. Jackson,	1907	H. Hinchcliffe, H. Rudstone,
	R. Crookes		Deyes
1885	L. Jackson,	1908	H. Hinchcliffe, H. Rudstone,
	A. Constable		H. Wrathall
1886	A. Constable	1909-1910	H. Rudstone, H. Wrathall
1887	A. Constable,	1911	F. W. Halliday
	Thompson	1912	F. W. Halliday, Wrightson
1888	H. Hill		

BEVERLEY C.C.

1852	Arnold	1871-1873	J. Burman
1853	C. Kenyon	1879	J. Brooks
1857	C. Kenyon	1880-1883	W. Kaye
1863	W. Hind	1884-1886	C. Boyes
1864	Parker	1887-1890	R. Wardell
1865	Caldecourt	1891	T. Blacker
1866	G. Drake	1892-1905	C. H. Mitchell
1867	C. Ullathorne	1912-1913	J. T. Green
1868	A. Crossland		

LONDESBOROUGH PARK C.C.

1862	Heseltine	1887-1894	W. Harbour,
1867	G. Wilson		A. Siddall
1868	Coxon	1895	W. Harbour
1871	Storey	1896	W. Harbour,
1872	Robinson		J. Falkiner
1885	T. Crossland	1897-1899	W. Harbour
1900-1902	W. Harbour		(Harbour was still playing in

146

| | A. Siddall |
| 1902 | W. Harbour |

1911. It is possible he was still the professional then.)

DRIFFIELD C.C.
1867	T. Brown
1893	B. Gledhill,
	J. W. Exley
1894-1895	A. Storer
1897	B. Hawkyard
1898-1899	H. Redden
1905	T. W. Gill
1906	F. Barker
1907-1908	T. Metcalfe
1909-1914	J. W. Teal

BRIDLINGTON C.C.
1865	Piper
1866-1867	J. W. Sagar
1893	J. Falkiner ?
1901-1905	J. Falkiner
1907-1908	J. Rollison
1912-1914	J. Rollison

HORNSEA C.C.
1872-1874	James Briggs
1875	T. Milnes
1876-1877	John Briggs
1878	E. Hodgkins
1879	J. K. Hughes
1895	W. G. Thompson

POCKLINGTON C.C.
| 1896-1897 | T. Mather |

HEDON WELLINGTON C.C.
| 1857 | Copson |
| 1860 | J. Mould |

MARKET WEIGHTON C.C.
| 1864 | J. Lister |

HUNMANBY MITFORD C.C.
(Professionals were often shared with Filey C.C. It is not always clear which club had first call on their services).

1882-1884	A. Smith	1895	W. Thompson
1885-1886	W. Thompson	1897-1898	A. Smith
1891	J. Ambler	1901	A. Smith
1892	J. Falkiner	1905	A. Smith
1893	W. Thompson		

FILEY C.C.
(See note on Hunmanby Mitford)

1888	W. Lamplough	1899-1900	F. White
1891	W. Simpson, J. Ambler,	1901	E. Horner
	J. Falkiner	1902	T. Woodhouse
1892	W. Simpson, F. Borton	1905-1906	T. Woodhouse
1893	F. Borton, T.E. Young,	1907	J. Garbutt
	F. Duckworth	1908	H. R. Laycock
1894	F. Borton, A. Smith,	1909	H. Atkinson
	W. Thompson	1910	T. Woodhouse
1895	W. Thompson	1914	A. Smith
1896	F. White		
1897-1898	H. Harrison		

147

APPENDIX TWO
VILLAGE CRICKET

There is no suggestion that the matches listed below were the first to be played in that village, merely that they are the first of which I have been able to find a record.

ALDBROUGH August 1863 v Roos
  Wright, Lickiss, Rawlinson, Prescott, Collinson, Kemp, Humble, Russell, Hardy, Small, Hutchinson.

ALLERTHORPE 1896 v Hayton
  R. Fenwick, T. Joy, J. Moor, F. G. Cains, C. Addinhall, G. C. Rudston, F. Futcher, W. Robson, J. Moor, C. G. Wellesley, J. Webster, W. G. Waterson.

ANLABY AND SKIDBY May 1856 v Welton
  G. Wilson, T. Lee, E. Clark, G. Davey, R. Good, F. Davey, J. Lee, H. Harrison, W. Wilson, R. Jefferson, T. Jefferson.

ATWICK 1871 v North Frodingham
  T. Wise, G. Malton, E. Storee, R. S. Cooper, J. G. Frost, T. Etherington, H. W. Smith, H. Myass, W. Frost, Rev. E. Gordon, E. Jessop.

AUGHTON 1897 v Melbourne
  Mr. Shaw, T. Townsley, Mr. Simpson, J. Sargant, W. J. Watson, G. Nutt, F. Anson, Mr. Newsome, B. Wake, W. Watson, C. Massam.

BAINTON August 1863 v Garton
  Perren, Oxtoby, Railton, Stevenson, J. Lee, Hill, H. Lee, Holdan, Range, Horsley, Richardson.

BARMBY MOOR 1895 v Wilberfoss
  H. Richardson, J. Moor, B. Moor, T. Wilson, A. Room, W. Wilkinson, B. Robson, H. Craven, A. Fountain, E. Wills, F. Carr.

BARMSTON August 1863 v Bridlington
  G. Reed give out 'took up the ball'.
  Carlton, Burdass, J. Carter, A. Hawe, G. Reed, Dawson, Harris, H. Reed. J. Stephenson, T. Stephenson, J. Chapman.

BEEFORD August 1870 v Skipsea
  J. Jamieson, F. Warren, H. Moorhouse, G. Smith, J. Agars, W. Medcalfe, E. Warren, Rev. W.G. Chilman, J. Marshall, W. Hought, W. Smith

148

BEMPTON July 1880 v Buckton
W. Cowton, C. Leppington, T. Rounding, L. Hought, A. S. Drake, A. Walmsley, F. Rounding, Lownsborough, W. Scott, T. Capes, C. Johnstone.

BIELBY 1895 v Hayton
F. Todd, J. Pippit, T. Lakin, H. Todd, G. Todd, J. Kendra, J. Johnson, J. Hill, R. Coverdale, W. Hill, C. Hayhurst.

BISHOP BURTON July 1857 v Cherry Burton
'The first game between the two sides'.
Ouston, Tomlinson, Watson, Ruddiforth, Wilson, Shepherd, Ellerington, Kennington, Horsefield, Duck, Dunn.

BISHOPTHORPE 1858 v Etton
A very professional side with several York players (*)
Scott*, Carr*, Napper*, Ferrand, Grimmer, Dewse*, Lofthouse*, Wake*, Cooke, Ades, Wright.

BISHOP WILTON August 1865 v Free Rangers
'The Thixendale drum and fife band was in attendance'.
T. Radge, H. Pearson, F. Wilson, A. Collinson, F. Coot, J. Foster, W. Wilson, H. Holderness, J. Pailing, J. Cook, W. Brown.

BRANDESBURTON August 1860 v Cherry Burton
W. Metcalfe, J. Metcalfe, W. Bilton, W. Clapham, W. Popple, J. Bilton, T. Marr, R. Jefferson, J. Charter, C. Bilton, H. Bateson.

BRANTINGHAM July 1868 v Cherry Burton
Beaumont, Whitehead, Barnby, Waltham, G. Wilson, F. Matthews, Palmer, Fearne, Miller, Smith, Chowler.

BROUGH 1878 v Welton 2nd Eleven

BUBWITH 1895 v Melbourne
T. Whitaker, J. Hatfield, J. Sayer, E. W. Harrison, J. Pratt, R. Hatfield, T. Newstead, C. Newstead, Blakey, W. Turner, H. Huby.

BUCKTON July 1880 v Bempton
T. Broadbent, T. Dixon, Hope, Bilton, J. Wiles, M. Cowton, C. Fenby, Hustler, May, Dunning, T. Jackson.

BURTON AGNES July 1879 v Carnaby
E. Myers, F. Mallory, J. Thwaites, F. Grainger, J. Cranswick, W. Smith, W. Taylor, P. Welburn, T. Taylor, W. Willis, S. Skelton.

BURTON CONSTABLE 1860 v Hull United
J. Smurthwaite, J. Wright, W. Hodgson, J. Trotter, W. Adamson, A. Bricknell, S. Burnett, T. Warwick, G. Parnell.

CARNABY July 1869 v Bridlington Excelsior
T. Cowman, S. Langdale, T. Bryan, T. Jackson, T. W. Clarke, G. Jackson, W. Lawler, H. Lightowler, G. Lightley, T. Reeveston, G. Horsley.

CHERRY BURTON July 1857 v Bishop Burton
'The first game between the two villages'.
Moody, Wilson, Thorley, Gabbetis, Stephenson, Cook, Everingham, W. Vickers, Stockdale, R. Vickers.

COTTAM August 1874 v Langtoft

COTTINGHAM July 1859 v Welton
Cpt. Farmer, Ed Wilson, Hubbersty, Jn. Binnington, W. Green, Jos. Harrison, G. Wilson, A. Coverdale, R. Donkin, R. Bearpark, R. Binnington.

CRANSWICK UNITED July 1876 v Beeford
J. Winter, J. Harvey, W. Merkin, W. Catton, G. Raynor, J. Garwood, G. Mathers, R. Sanderson, R. Gowthorpe, T. Catton, T. Wilkinson.,

DALTON HOLME 1873 v Kiplingcotes
G. Clowes, J. Marshall, G. Hilvington, F. Wright, J. Kemp, T. Hope, G. Burns, W. Sachell, J. Simpson, W. Atkinson.

DUGGLEBY September 1888 v Sledmere
Duggleby's first ever (?) match. They had 9 left handed batsmen and were 8 all out before taking tea at the Triton.
C. Merry, E. Ringrose, G. Cawood, T. Milner, J. Fox, A. Bogg, E. Warters, R. Fletcher, T. Warters, R. Burdett, H. Brown.

EAST COTTINGWORTH 1900 v Melbourne
Fratson, T. Room, Craven, T. Hawe, W. Room, J. Thompson, J. Brown, B. Pears, J. Houseman, J. Room, Rickatson.

EBBERSTON July 1866 v Foxholes

ELLERKER 1862 v North Ferriby
Rev. J. Waltham, T. F. Waltham, R. Waltham, E. Waltham, M. Munroe, F. Wilson, H. Pearson, Oxtoby, Allison, Wilson, F. Smith.

ETTON July 1856 v Anlaby
R. Whipp, Pottage, W. Pickard, Bew, J. Whipp, J. Pickard, Crosby, R. Welbourn, Morris, Barker.

EVERINGHAM 1896 v Melbourne
C. Johnson, J. Lee, T. Cook, F. Johnson, W. Norwood, A. Brown, J. Miller, W. Robson, P. Cook, W. Breighton, J. Miller.

FANGFOSS 1895 v Bishop Wilton
A. Prest, Dales, Hodgson, Prest, Yardley, Campling, Grisewood, Atkinson, Bielby, Hodgson, Clint.

FERRIBY June 1872 v Cherry Burton
G. Everingham, B. Harrison, R. Ledley, C. Kirtland, Dunn, Rev. Ellis, J. Kirtland, J. Spilman, E. Bearpark, Clark, Spilman.

FLAMBOROUGH September 1863 v Bridlington
R. Crowe, W. Whytehead, F. Chew, T. Woodhouse, B. Sawden, W. Woodhouse, J. Brooks, R. Sawden, M. Bailey, J. Traves, G. Hall.

FOXHOLES July 1860 v Langtoft

FRIDAYTHORPE September 1892 v Pocklington
C. J. Young, J. Hardy, H. Young, G. Johnson, T. Lakin, F. Cook, T. Atkinson, G. Railton, B. Barker, M. Cole, J. Adams.

GANTON August 1863 v Sherburn
Franks, Robson, Walker, D. W. Legard Esq., Sir F. D. Legard, Robinson, Ringrose, Langton, Pickering, Beswick, Dalby.

GARROWBY 1899 v Warter
R. Hick, T. Fletcher, W. Asberry, T. Smith, H. L. Boyes, J. Binge, J. Boyes, T. Webster, G. Gospel, C. Clarke, H. Boyes.

GARTON June 1860 v Lund
'being the first cricket match that was ever played in that village'.
W. Botterill, Howden, J. Crust, Neighbour, T. Crust, Hopper, A. Botterill, Larkins, J. Crust, J. Crust (!) E. Piercey.

GOODMANHAM June 1885 v Dalton Holme
W. Usher, R. Newbald, W. Brown, J. Wreghitt, W. Hurd, G. Cobb, H. Usher, H. Camm, T. Marshall, T. Withell, G. Cooper.

HALSHAM July 1864 v Roos
F. Gibson, T. Watson, J. Fewson, W. Whisker, A. Gibson, A. Fewson, Thorpe, Richardson, Duke, Wright, M. Whisker.

HARPHAM August 1898 v Nafferton
W. Theakstone, H. Day, W. Milner, L. Owston, G. Harrison, G. Brewster, C. Kilvington, W. Milbank, T. Fields, C. Thrower, C. Thornton.

HAYTON 1895 v Bielby
H. Johnson, F. Norwood, H. Welbourne, R. Wilkinson, H. Dixon, H. Kendall, J. Richardson, W. Holden, W. Hewson, W. Wilson, H. Hill.

HELPERTHORPE 1871 v Weaverthorpe
J. Passey, J. Heslerton, W. Adams, R. Harland, G. Elliott, G. Grice, T. Bean, R. Brookes, R. Robinson, J. Bell, T. Thompson.

HOLME-ON-SPALDING MOOR September 17th 1861 v Seaton Ross
Ogram, Marshall, Blackburn, Tyler, Hope, Amos, Cook, Whitehead, Clark, Sanderson, Bradley.

HOLMPTON July 1877 v Welwick

HOTHAM August 1862 v Cherry Burton
Brown, Needham, - Beaumont Esq., Cpt. Fox, Jackson, Newbould, Oxtoby, Goodliffe, Stather, Hallam, Gooseman.

HUGGATE August 1869 v Wetwang

HUMBLETON 1851
First Annual General Meeting. No details.

KILHAM July 1868 v Rudston
T. Ward, Watt, T. Gardham, Rickinson, T. H. Harrison, W. Ricketson, F. Hodgson, S. Wilson, Haggitt, Lamplugh, Smith.

KILNWICK August 1860 v Watton
Leadill, Wise, Duggleby, Oldroyd, Davis, Kemp, Owston, Brigham - Duggleby, - Davis, Hanson.

KIPLINGCOTES July 1873 v Dalton Holme
H. Towse, J. S. Riley, E. J. Riley, T. Spence, G. Riley, J. Hart, Cooper, J. Allen, Egiston, Hoggard. (10 men only).

KIRBYUNDERDALE 1902 v Wetwang
Fletcher, Hicks, G. Smith, Bings, Harper, Clark, Monkman, Johnson, Wilkinson, Jennings, J. Hope.

KIRKELLA 1860 v Tranby
T. Lee, J. Lee, W. Lee, E. Whitaker, G. Wilson, O. Wilkinson, J. Binnington, R. Binnington, G. Edwards, S. Voase, T. Morehead.

LANGTOFT July 1860 v Garton
Carter, - Gardiner, R. H. Brown, W. Brown, C. Lamplugh, Rev. C. Day, H. Woodmansey, Duggleby, Gardiner, T. Woodmansey, W. Lamplugh.

LEVEN 1871 v Routh
F. Calvert, J. Dennison, R. Hebb, Rev. F. Beadell, Moore, R. Sanders, W. H. Sanders, E. Wright, R. Dooks, Blenkin, Darbyshire.

LOCKINGTON June 1870 v Brandesburton (a return match)
R. Hardy, J. Smith, H. Duggleby, D. Everingham, W. Nicholson, J. Ireland, Wood, Blakeston, Clark, T. Duggleby.

LOWTHORPE 1890 v Scampston
G. A. Pearson, T. Jefferson, E. Allen, Rev. V. G. Daltry, J. C. Lamplough, J. G. Frankish, C. Crompton, M. Piercey, J. Medforth, W. Robinson, F. O. Piercey.

LUND 1859 v North Frodingham
S. Vary, H. Ford, T. Stephenson, G. Lyon, R. Ford, T. Norman, R. Simpson, W. Crosby, Bew, M. Chapman, R. Grubb.

MARKET WEIGHTON 1852 v Howden
Scaife, S. Young, Sanderson, Sayner, Kent, Pearse, Jowse, Jobson, J. Young, Wake, Hewson.

MARTON and SEWERBY 1871 v Kilham

MELBOURNE 1895 v Warter
F. Todd, J. Robson, A. Gibson, A. Cragg, J. Johnson, G. Todd, H. Richardson, T. Harrison, G. Homley, H. Todds, J. Parker.

MIDDLETON 1856 v Etton
In the grounds of the Rectory at Middleton.
Cass, Foster, Rev. E. J. Hitchings, W. Crosby, Ford, Park, Rev. J. Blanchard, Lotherington, Norman, Vary, Crowe.

MUSTON May 1872 v Hunmanby
Hartley, Barmby, White, Hudson, Marshall, Boyes, Hall, Woodhouse, Bennison, Fenwick, England.

NAFFERTON July 1864 v Garton
Wilkinson, Holtby, Robson, Sugden, Lovel, Whittaker, Broadley, Holgraves, Crompton, Hoggard, Goodwill.

NORTH BURTON July 1870 v Foxholes
W. Foster, M. Hall, W. Major, W. Mallory, J. Brown, M. Danby, T. Young, Brown, R. Ingham, Hartley, W. Nixon.

NORTH FERRIBY 1862 v Ellerker
Cpt. Thackery, J. Bearpark, Bradley, Rev. C. N. Wawne, Levenden, J. Stephenson, E. Wiley, G. Everingham, W. Knowles, E. Pettingell, R. V. Knowles.

NORTH FRODINGHAM 1859 v Lund
W. Metcalf, R. Baron, J. Idell, J. Metcalf, B. Pepper, J. Baron, T. Allman, J. Wilson, J. Atkinson, W. Petch, W. Bilton.

OTTRINGHAM June 1877 v Patrington
W. Jackson, W. Blenkin, A. Quilter, T. Hodgson, W. Jackson, J. Garton, H. Pawson, R. Grayburn, E. Hutchinson, G. Jackson, R. Woodmansey.

PATRINGTON 1851
A new club formed. No details.

RISE 1859 v Beverley Young Freeman
W. Robinson, W. Palin, W. Okney, S. Clappeson, M. Robinson, T. Maud, J. Ogg, J. Robinson, E. Browning, J. Robson, W. Killington.

ROOS Albion August 1860 v Burton Constable
G. Harland, E. Evans, D. Fairbank, H. Tate, W. Harland, J. Batty, W. Fewson, J. Fewson, Shenton, Jubb, E. Elam.

ROUTH 1871 v Leven
R. Turnbull, T. Jackson, Harland Whiting, C. H. Whiting, J. Whiting, W. Jackson, C. Waltham, W. Barber, T. Hick, P. Pease.

RUDSTON June 1868 v Ganton.
'The monotony of Rudston was materially relieved last week by the announcement that a cricket match would be played in that village'.
Rev. H. S. Watson, Thurlow, G. Hewson, R. Teal, W. Dunn, W. Foster, T. Foster, Ward, Gregory, Guardham, Brigham.

SALTMARSHE AND WALLINGFEN 1788 v Howden

154

SCAMPSTON June 1861 v Sledmere
Lamb, R. Walles, Lightowler, Pennington, Douglass, Tipling, Botterill, T. Wallis, Warwick, Pateman, Neate.

SEATON ROSS 17th September 1861 v Holme-on-Spalding Moor
Smith, Moore, Farmery, Fenghill, Walker, J. Brighton, Adamson, M. Brighton, Pratt, Rook, Sanderson.

SETTRINGTON June 1891 v Weaverthorpe
J. Sturdy, M. Blackwell, W. Kitching, J. Boyes, G. Bielby, R. Lotherington, J. Walker, J. Wilson, A. Rice, F. Bielby, F. Fergusson.

SEWERBY AND FLAMBOROUGH 1864 v Bridlington
J. Lythe, L. Lythe, B. Simpson, H. Milner, Brookes, Plaxton, B. Simpson, R. Crowe, G. D. Watson, W. Perfect, J. Dixon.

SHERBURN August 1863 v Ganton
Durham, J. Bielby, Willoughby, Pinkney, Rev. J. Mason, Anderson, Bielby, Allen, Jackson, Bedell, Hodgson.

SIGGLESTHORNE July 1859 v Hornsea at Wassand
W. Taylor, C. Wheatley, W. Nutchere, Girdley, Idell, F. Clarke, Whitno, R. Morley, Bateson, Lockey (10 men).

SKIDBY June 1863 v Cottingham
O. Voase, A. Hutchinson, R. Kirk, W. Wood, W. Lee, S. Voase, A. Voase, T. Jefferson, R. Waslin, H. Waslin.

SKIPSEA September 1865 v Barmston
J. Frankish, J. Stork, W. Green, C. Walker, F. Robinson, J. Botham, A. Farman, C. Chadwick, T. Baker, C. Godfrey.

SKIRLAUGH 1860 v Beverley
Job Smith, W. Hobson, J. L. Smith, S. Sherwood, H. Bell, R. Richardson, M. Robson, J. Robinson, P. Newton, G. Lickiss, M. Lickiss.

SLEDMERE June 1861 v Scampston
Neighbour, M. Hope, Potts, Train, Crust, Marshall, Hesp, Hardy, J. Hope, Douthwaite, Bell.

SNAINTON May 1866 v Bridlington
J. King, J. Thompson, G. Watson, Beswick, J. Allison, Rose, J. Cooper, Railton, Spence, Matthews, Hutchinson.

SOUTHBURN 1904 v Cranswick
P. Brown, W. Leason, W. Dale, G. Johnson, A. Leason, M. Hartley, J. Binnington, W. Scott, J. Binnington, H. Simpson, J. Sewter.

SOUTH CAVE July 1863 v Cherry Burton
Littlewood, Howard, Oxtoby, Bilton, Waltham, Pearson, Westmoreland, Wride, Smith.

SOUTH DALTON 1874 v Etton
S. Hoggard, J. Allen, W. Atkinson, W. Garforth, E. King, W. Acaster, J. Voase, D. Crocket, R. Hardy, J. Sutherland, G. Kilvington.

SOUTH FERRIBY September 1862 v North Ferriby
'The underhand bowling of Mucklow, Skelton and Gibson was very good and seemed to puzzle their opponents'.
Skelton, Fowler, Berridge, Mucklow, Parkin, Franklin, Gibson, Wadingham, Hembrough, Dent, Newbald.

SOUTHBURN June 1900 v Lund
T. Beall, B. Wilson, J. Binnington, E. Hudson, J. Sewter, Col. Staveley, W. Hartley, M. J. Nicholls, J. Noble, W. Sharp, W. Foster.

SPROATLEY June 1861 v Burton Constable
W. Bell, W. Hotham, A. Mercer, D. Lound, J. Milburne, J. Horner, S. Horsman, G. Lound, J. Fairbank, E. Heron, R. Earles.

STAXTON May 1879 v Foxholes
J. Lister, T. Flinton, J. Bielby, S. Glaves, T. Flinton, F. Bielby, T. Spavin, G. Dobson, W. Dobson, F. Dobson, Dr. Dodd.

SUTTON June 1866 v Hull United
Fawcett, Kidd, (Both borrowed from Hull Kingston C.C.) S. Ross, Cooke, Hall, Rodmell, H. Ross, Batley, Catis, Whitehead, Davis.

SUTTON ON DERWENT 1896 v Marlborough
F. Vause, Mr. Woods, Cpt. Simpson, Hon. R. Jarvis, Giles, Mayor Heron, B. Richardson, W. Midgley, R. Waldy, Harper, Mr. Botterill.

SWINE 1877 v South Myton
H. Horner, C. Clary, S. Sherwood, E. Fawbert, J. T. Palin, Robinson, Iago, B. Weatherill, T. Sherwood, S. Chatterton, Holt.

THWING AND WOLD NEWTON June 1886 v North Burton
S. Southwell, J. Burdass, T. Southwell, C. Kitchen, W. Hick, R. Lamplough, T. Schoolmaster, C. Morris, C. Hope, T. Redhead, J. Lowish.

TIBTHORPE 1871 v Bainton
A. Staveley, J. Woodcock, A. Botterill, J. Horsley, G. Allen, J. Foster, J. Clark, A. Foster, R. Clark, H. Staveley, W. Woodcock.

WALKINGTON June 1892 v Bishop Burton
J. A. Mathison, T. Ford, R. Dunning, G. Leaper, G. Thorpe, J. Wilson, W. Stainton, M. Leaper, W. Holmes, R. Northend, S. Wilson.

WARTER August 1872 v Brantingham
A. Macauley, J. Storey, Welsby, H. Usher, Rev. Barber, Watson, Blearley, E. Usher, W. Rickell, J. Clarke.

WATTON August 1860 v Kilnwick
Moody, Maltby, Harvey, Knoles, Perfect, Clark, Moody, Nicholson, Lamb, Tune, Tadman.

WAWNE AND MEAUX July 1868 v Sutton
Wyndham, Kelly, R. Turnbull, R. Calvert, R. Scott, Myers, F. Calvert, Rev. E. J. Henslowe, H. Whiting, T. Boville, M. Jackson.

WEAVERTHORPE 1858 v Driffield
Jas. Mason, W. Bellwood, R. Anderson, G. Anderson, J. Bell, J. Ringrose, Jno. Mason, J. Barber, G. Lovell, (plus two).

WELWICK July 1877 v Holmpton

WELTON 1854 v Hull Mechanics' Institute
Wilson, Parker, Carver, Raikes, J. K. Watson, Sadler, Ward, W. Watson, J. Pease, Smith, Leaper.

WEST LUTTON August 1872 v Weaverthorpe
H. Train, G. Hill, T. Marfleet, J. Thelwell, W. Train, G. Wood, J. Train, W. Milner, J. Duck, T. Russell, W. Ness.

WETWANG July 1864 'several members of the Beverley and Garton clubs' v Driffield Albert Club
W. Lakin, W. Blowman, J. Blowman, C. Blowman, H. Thellwell, J. Wilson, W. Chambers, B. Cappleman, J Crust, J. Hopper, J. Neighbour.

WESTON August 1885 v Weaverthorpe
W. Topham, F. Hepton, T. Oliver, T. Rivis, H. Hoggard, G. Fletcher, T. Fletcher, R. Luddrington, W. Clapham, S. Calam, T. Hodgson.

WILBERFOSS August 1880 v Warter at Bishop Wilton
A. Siddall, G. Wilson, R. Ringrose, T. Allison, T. Lister, W. Donkin, R. Smith, G. Jennings, W. Ward, R. Hurwell, W. Usher.

WILLERBY June 1865 v Hull Institute
Lee, Hardy, Binnington, Towers, Wood, Ferraby, Fawcett, Moorehead, Harden, Waltham, Fowler.

WITHERNSEA and Vistors September 1862 v Hull Kingston
(Hull had nine players barred when the match was arranged)
Hewitt, Iveson, Shaw, Barton, Galloway, Toogood, Biglin, McManus, Coleman, Skelton, Barnfather.

WOLD NEWTON July 1880 v North Burton
J. Cadman, S. Southwell, C. Bartlett, J. Harlann, W. Hicks, J. Burdass, T. Hicks, F. Ullyott, J. Redshaw, W. Bannister, J. Duggleby.

158

APPENDIX THREE

The choice of score-cards in this appendix has been made on the basis of including as many early cards as possible. An attempt has been made to include 'first' or 'early' matches for some of the town clubs, as well as some of the more interesting representative matches.

ELEVEN OFFICERS OF THE 4th AND 5th WEST YORKSHIRE REGTS.

v

TEN OFFICERS OF REGIMENTS ENCAMPED IN HOLDERNESS
Played at the cricket ground in this town (Hull) — 3rd August 1798

4th AND 5th WEST YORKSHIRE

1st Innings			2nd Innings	
Mr. Paris	3	b Lennox	1	b Coast
Mr. Walker	0	b Coast	2	c Musters
Cpt. Smithsen	2	c Lennox	0	c Lennox
Cpt. Wilson	4	run out	2	b Lennox
Mr. Reed	0	st Lennox	0	st Lennox
J. E. Smith	29	c Coast	0	c Yorke
Mjr. Brandling	26	b Musters	15	b Lennox
Cpt. Lee	1	c Coast	2	run out
Mr. Totie	0	b Musters	2	c Musters
Sir C. Turner	0	c Musters	1	run out
Mr. Jackson	0	notched out	2	not out
Extras	9		4	Extras
	72		31	

THE 10 OFFICERS		1st Innings		2nd Innings
Mj.Gen Lennox	19	b Paris	5	b Brandling
Cpt. Musters	39	b Brandling	14	run out
Cpt. Clay	6	b Reed	27	c Lee
Mjr. Marriott	3	c Walker	1	run out
Mr. Coast	6	b Paris	10	b Reed
Mr. Worship	7	b Brandling	1	b Brandling
Mr. Wallace	2	not out	0	b Reed
Mr. Williams	1	c Wilson	2	c Wilson
Mr. Strenton	2	b Paris	16	b Reed
Mr. York	3	b Brandling	14	not out
Extras	12		14	Extras
	100		104	

This is the earliest score-card for a match played in the East Riding. 'Mr. Jackson notched out' may be a printer's error for 'not out'.

ALL ENGLAND ELEVEN v HULL AND DISTRICT
19th, 20th and 21st July 1849

ALL ENGLAND: 1st Innings

Chatterton	c Morgan	b Parker	29
Hinkley	c Morgan	b Lambert	1
Parr	c Lister	b Lambert	14
F. Pilch		b Parker	52
A. Mynn Esq.	c Lead	b Parker	14
N. Felix Esq.		b Parker	49
Guy	c Morgan	b Parker	6
H. W. Lindow Esq.		b Taylor	10
Clarke	c Potts	b Taylor	2
Wynne Esq.	c Allington	b Taylor	3
Bickley	not out		31
	Byes 3; wide balls 28		31
			212

HULL AND DISTRICT: 1st Innings / 2nd Innings

	1st Innings			2nd Innings		
W. J. Lunn	run out		0	c Mynn	b Bickley	0
Parker	run out		2	c Parr	b Clarke	0
C. P. Loft	c Felix	b Clarke	13		b Bickley	0
Lead		b Bickley	2	c Parr	b Clarke	1
W. Marshall	c Chatterton	b	0		b Clarke	2
Lt. Lake	c Mynn	b Bickley	0		b Bickley	0
Bowlby		b Bickley	11		b Clarke	4
Bickers	lbw	b Bickley	12	c Lindow	b Bickley	1
Morgan	run out	Chatterton	1		b Clarke	0
W. V. Grantham	run out	Chatterton	0	lbw	b Bickley	0
R. Allington		b Clarke	0		b Clarke	2
Potts	c Bickley	b Clarke	3	c Lindow	b Bickley	13
Lt. Godby		b Bickley	6	not out		13
Lister	c Felix	b Bickley	1		b Clarke	0
Wheatley		b Clarke	2		b Clarke	0
W. Lambert		b Bickley	0		b Clarke	12
J. H. Taylor		b Bickley	0		b Clarke	1
R. Hewitt		b Clarke	3	st Chatterton		19
G. Bentley		b Bickley	3	st Chatterton		0
R. Wake	run out		2		b Bickley	2
W. C. Robinson		b Bickley	0		b Bickley	2
E. Casson	st Chatterton		0	S. Fisher	lbw	0
	w2, b2		4	w2, b3		5
			65			65

ST. GEORGE'S 1st XI v HULL ATHENAEUM 2nd XI
10th August 1849

HULL ATHENAEUM: 1st Innings   2nd Innings

Haire	st by Ayre	b Prissick	10		b Galloway	5
Coverdale		b Prissick	7		b Galloway	7
Bew		b Prissick	0		b Prissick	8
James Glover		b Prissick	0		b Galloway	1
Milson		b Galloway	0		b Prissick	0
Prest	b Galloway	c Frost	3		b Prissick	0
Jackson	b Prissick	c Frankish	3		b Prissick	19
Fisher		b Prissick	4	lbw	b Prissick	1
Kitching	not out		9	lbw	b Galloway	7
Vause	b Prissick	c Harrison	4	c Frost	b Galloway	1
Morris		b Galloway	0	not out		1
b2, w1			3	b2, w1		3
			43		(sic!)	55

ST. GEORGE'S: 1st Innings   2nd Innings

Watson	b Haire	c Prest	1	c Milson	b Haire	2
Ryland	b Kitching	c Jackson	3		b Kitching	6
Harrison		b Kitching	0	not out		4
Galloway		b Kitching	8		b Haire	9
F. Ayre	b Kitching	c Bew	0		b Kitching	1
Frankish		b Haire	3		b Haire	17
Carter	b and c	Kitching	0	c Milson	b Kitching	3
Prissick	c Glover	b Haire	8		b Kitching	0
Frost	not out		6	st Jackson	b Haire	2
C. Ayre	c Prest	b Kitching	0	c Prest	b Haire	6
E. Dryden		b Haire	0		b Kitching	0
Extras			0	Extras		0
			29			50

Hull Athenaeum won by 19 runs (17 runs!)

161

ST. GEORGE'S v HULL KINGSTON
1850

ST. GEORGE'S: 1st Innings   2nd Innings

F. Ayre		b J. B. Mould	3	c		b Mould	4
A. Frost		b Mould	1	lbw			2
E. Wawne		b Mould	0			b Mould	2
W. Prest	lbw		4	c		b Mould	0
F. M. Casson	c	b Islip	6	st by Groves			0
G. Whittaker	c	b Cattley	2				
J. B. Fea		b Mould	0				
G. Kitching	c	b Islip	1			b Mould	2
T. Frankish	lbw		0	not out			2
C. E. Ayre	not out		0				
J. Malcolm		b Mould	0			b Mould	0
4w, 10b, 11b			15	1w, 8b, 41b			13
			32			7 for	25

HULL KINGSTON: 1st Innings

C. Stuart		b Prest	3
Jackson	run out		0
J. K. Haire		b Prest	14
B. Groves	c	b Fea	51
J. M. Taylor	c and	b Prest	60
T. H. Mould	lbw		17
Cade		b Prest	3
W. Islip		b Prest	0
A. Cattley		b Prest	0
Colley	st by Casson		3
J. B. Mould	not out		9
16w, 3nb, 29b			48
			208

This is a high scoring game for the period. Hull Kingston were the premier side in the city and St. George's was a junior club.

162

HULL KINGSTON v BEVERLEY
In the field of Kingston C.C. 1850

BEVERLEY: 1st Innings				2nd Innings		
Race	b and	c T. H. Mould	8	c J. Mould	b T.H. Mould	15
Wallis		b F. Ayre	15	b and	c T. Mould	2
Feast		b T. H. Mould	8	lbw	b Ayre	0
Taylor		b T. H. Mould	0		b Ayre	3
Bickers		b Ayre	1	c Lunn	b Ayre	2
Priestley	b and	c T. H. Mould	0	not out		1
Hall	c Haire	b T. H. Mould	5		b Ayre	3
Westoboy	b and	c T. H. Mould	1		b Ayre	2
Hallewell			3		b Ayre	1
Earle	not out		2	c T.H. Mould	b Ayre	12
Musgrave		b T. H. Mould	2	c Groves	b Ayre	0
Extras			6	Extras		4
			49			45

HULL KINGSTON:		1st Innings	
B. Groves	c Taylor	b Earle	39
F. Ayre	c	b Bickers	0
J. K. Haire	run out		5
Feast		b Bickers	6
J. H. Taylor	c Musgrave	b Earle	8
R. Hewitt		b Earle	15
T. H. Mould	c Taylor	b Bickers	0
Bowlby	c	b Bickers	0
Dr. Casson	not out		5
Dr. Lunn	run out		2
J. B. Mould		b Bickers	4
Extras			10
			99

Hull Kingston won by an innings and 5 runs.

163

HOWDEN v ST. GEORGE'S
1851

HOWDEN: 1st Innings

2nd Innings

Ullathorne	c	b Frankish	13		b H. Ayre	0
Taylor		b Prissick	1	run out		1
Bussey		b F. Ayre	3	c	b F. Ayre	1
Jackson		b Prissick	7		b Prissick	0
Clark	c	b Prissick	2		b F. Ayre	3
Fletcher	c	b Wake	1		b F. Ayre	1
Robinson		b F. Ayre	3	c	b Kitching	0
Saltmarshe		b Prissick	8	lbw		3
Fleming		b F. Ayre	2	lbw		1
Lambe	not out		0	c	b Prissick	8
Shepherd		b F. Ayre	1	not out		0
Extras			13	Extras		4
			54			29

ST. GEORGE'S: 1st Innings

2nd Innings

Prissick	lbw	b Fletcher	4	lbw	b Fletcher	3
F. Ayre	lbw	b Bussey	0	lbw	b Fletcher	2
Kitching	run out	b Bussey	7		b Fletcher	1
Wake		b Bussey	0		b Fletcher	10
Frankish		b Fletcher	1		b Fletcher	0
Harrison	c Fleming	b Fletcher	10	not out	Fletcher (sic)	4
Frost		b Bussey	2		b Fletcher	4
H. Ayre		b Frankish	0		b Saltmarshe	0
Carter	not out	b Frankish (sic)	2		b Frankish	1
Stephenson		b Saltmarshe	3		b Frankish	0
Bielby		b Frankish	0		b Frankish	1
Extras			11	Extras		5
			40			31

Howden won by 12 runs.

Umpires: C. Houldsworth (Howden) Mr. Loft (Hull).
'The slow dodging bowling of Mr. Prissick' caused Howden problems. One Hull batsman was warned about 'giving way to such an extent to the violence of his feelings' when given out.

ALL-ENGLAND ELEVEN v BEVERLEY AND DISTRICT
9th, 10th and 11th August, 1852

ALL-ENGLAND: 1st Innings				2nd Innings		
J. Caesar	c Morton		4			
T. Adams		b Wright	24	not out		2
J. Guy	c Shepherd		4		b Tinley	0
G. Parr	c Morton		4		b Wright	1
T. Box	c Scott		13	run out		0
W. Caffin		b Wright	0	c Coates		6
G. Anderson	c Arnold		0	run out		22
W. Martingell	c Shepherd		2	not out		0
N. Felix	c Shepherd		2			
J. Bickley		b Tinley	1	c Bickers		0
W. Clarke	not out		0			
b1, w5			6	b1, w1		2
			60		6 for	33

BEVERLEY AND DISTRICT: 1st Innings

C. Peach	run out		0
C. H. Priestley		b Bickley	9
H. Maister		b Bickley	1
H. Wright (pro)		b Bickley	0
T. Scott		b Bickley	0
A. Shepherd	c Bickley		7
W. Abbey		b Clarke	0
J. Walker	run out		2
M. Stainsby	st Box		9
R. Bickers	st Box		6
C. Arnold (pro)	not out		25
F. Tinley (pro)		b Bickley	0
F. Casson	c Parr		1
F. Wallace	c Bickley		0
H. I. Earle	c Parr		1
J. Coates	c Caesar		15
G. Morton		b Martingell	0
W. Scott		b Martingell	0
F. H. Brown	c Bickley		0
J. Westerby		b Clarke	0
J. Musgrave		b Clarke	1
I. A. D'Olier		b Clarke	0
b1, lb3, w1			5
			82

BRIDLINGTON v SCARBOROUGH
Played at Bridlington, 11th May 1852

SCARBOROUGH: 1st Innings / 2nd Innings

Batsman	1st dismissal	1st runs	2nd dismissal	2nd runs
Holt	run out	3	c by Shaw	21
A. McKintosh	c by Taylor	3	b Carr	5
Jackson	c by Taylor	4	c by Hind	1
J. Mackereth	c by Carr	9	b Stanton	0
Benson	b Carr	2	b Carr	0
Kohler	run out	2	not out	14
Sharpin	not out	21	b Carr	0
Revell	b Taylor	14	b Carr	1
Horner	c by Rycroft	1	b Stanton	1
Reed	b Carr	0	c by Barker	5
Bell	b Carr	3	c by Harland	3
Extras	2b, 1nb	3	5b, 5w	10
		65		66

BRIDLINGTON: 1st Innings / 2nd Innings

Batsman	1st dismissal	1st runs	2nd dismissal	2nd runs
Stanton	st by Mackereth	0	lbw	0
Cranswick	c and b Mackereth	6	c by Bell	4
W. Barker	b Mackereth	13	not out	10
Carr	b Mackereth	4	c by Holt	3
Taylor	c by Mackereth	7	hit wicket	0
Shaw	run out	0		
Harland	b Benson	17		
R. Barker	b Benson	51		
Hind	b Bell	0		
Baker	b Benson	0		
Rycroft	not out	0		
Extras	3b, 1nb, 10w	14	4w	4
		112		4 for 21

Bridlington won by 6 wickets.

This is the earliest Bridlington score-card. Bowlers were not always given credit for catches and lbw's off their bowling, particularly if there was a wager involved. Note Mackereth's 3 wickets and a stumping in the same Bridlington innings.

166

DRIFFIELD v BURLINGTON
Played at Shady Lane, Driffield, 7th July 1855

DRIFFIELD: 1st Innings ... **2nd Innings**

Batsman	1st Innings			2nd Innings		
Eddowes	lbw		0	c Franks	b W. Savage	2
Burton		b W. Savage	3		b J. Savage	9
Harrison		b J. Savage	0	run out		0
Lydon	hit wicket		0		b J. Savage	5
Fawcett		b J. Savage	4	lbw		0
Lumb		b W. Savage	3		b W. Savage	0
Shaw		b W. Savage	1		b J. Savage	1
Botterill		b W. Savage	11		b J. Savage	1
Clark		b J. Savage	0		b W. Savage	0
Hornby	not out		0	lbw		0
Kirkby	lbw		0	not out		6
Extras	5b, 4w		9	3w		3
			31			**44**

BURLINGTON: 1st Innings ... **2nd Innings**

Batsman	1st Innings			2nd Innings		
W. Savage		b Harrison	12		b Burton	0
Franks		b Burton	2	c Shaw		2
W. Barker		b Eddowes	6	st Fawcett		2
R. Barker		b Burton	1	c Lumb	b Harrison	0
J. Savage		b Hornby	0		b Botterill	13
Preston	run out		0	c Harrison	b Lydon	5
Armitage		b Burton	0		b Lydon	2
E. H. Lamplugh	not out		0		b Burton	5
Machen		b Harrison	0	not out		5
Latrobe		b Harrison	0	c Shaw	b Harrison	5
J. Lamplugh		b Burton	3	c Burton	b Harrison	4
Extras	2b		2	2b 4nb		6
			26			**49**

The match ended in a tie.

This is the earliest score-card for Driffield. Frank Lydon was a Royal Academician, Benjamin Fawcett a distinguished engraver. No doubt they both batted artistically.

167

11 GENTLEMEN OF POCKLINGTON v 11 GENTLEMEN OF BEVERLEY
Played at Pocklington 1857

POCKLINGTON: 1st Innings / 2nd Innings

Name	1st dismissal	1st bowler	1st runs	2nd dismissal	2nd bowler	2nd runs
Kilby		b Wyberg	3	c Palmer	b Walker	4
A. Morris	c Palmer	b Wyberg	3	c and	b Walker	10
H. Silburn	not out		10		b Walker	2
Blanchard	c Pottage	b Wyberg	23	c Pottage	b Earle	1
Wright		b Wyberg	18	st Musgrave	b Earle	4
Wray	run out		1	c Hall	b Earle	2
W. Silburn		b Wyberg	2	c Hutton	b Earle	0
Gilbertson	c Hutton	b Musgrave	2	run out		5
Forth	c Palmer	b Wyberg	1	not out		7
R. Morris		b Musgrave	2	run out		0
Extras 14w, 7b, 3lb			24	Extras 7w, 5b, 3lb		15
			104			56

BEVERLEY: 1st Innings / 2nd Innings

Name	1st dismissal	1st bowler	1st runs	2nd dismissal	2nd bowler	2nd runs
Wyberg		b Blanchard	4		b Blanchard	0
Beaumont		b Blanchard	12		b Blanchard	17
Walker		b Wright	5		b Blanchard	2
Pottage	c Silburn	b Wright	24	c Blanchard	b Morris	0
Musgrave	not out		3	c Morris	b Blanchard	14
Hallewell		b Blanchard	2	not out		20
Hutton	run out		13	not out		8
Palmer		b Blanchard	3			
Hall	lbw		9			
Earle		b Blanchard	5			
Duesbery		b Harrison	2			
Extras 2w, 7b			9	Extras 5w, 2b, 2nb		9
			91			5 for 70

Beverley won by 5 wickets.

168

HORNSEA v SIGGLESTHORNE
Played at Wassand 23rd July 1859

SIGGLETHORNE:

	1st Innings			2nd Innings		
W. Taylor		b Thorley	2	c Grantham	b Thorley	0
C. Wheatley	run out		0		b Rose	5
W. Nutchere	c Scott	b Rose	1		b Thorley	0
Girdley		b Thorley	4	c Rose	b Thorley	15
Idell	c Heslop	b Thorley	0		b Rose	10
F. Clarke		b Rose	0		b Rose	5
Whitno	not out		4	hit wkt	b Rose	13
R. Morley	c Grantham	b Thorley	1	c Rose	b Thorley	0
Bateson	c Rose	b Thorley	0	not out		3
Lockey		b Rose	3		b Thorley	7
Extras			0	Extras		5
			18			70

HORNSEA:

	1st Innings			2nd Innings		
J. Rose	c Lockey	b Whitno	2	c Nutcher	b Whitno	13
R. Holt	run out		4	hit wkt	b Whitno	6
S. Heslop		b Wheatley	0	c Girdley	b Whitno	3
D. Thorley		b Wheatley	8	hit wkt	b Whitno	0
J. Scott		b Wheatley	12		b Wheatley	3
J. Line		b Whitno	6	not out		4
G. Coates	hit wkt		6		b Whitno	1
W. Knaggs		b Whitno	0	not out		6
T. Grantham		b Wheatley	8			
W. Southwick	lbw		1			
G. Peers	not out		1			
Extras			3	Extras		2
			51			6 for 38

Hornsea won by 4 wickets.

This is the first recorded match for Hornsea.

POCKLINGTON v DRIFFIELD
Played at Pocklington, Friday 15th June, 1860

POCKLINGTON: 1st Innings   2nd Innings

Wilkinson	lbw	Seaton	23	c Teal	b Day	5
Smallpiece	c Matthews	b Day	2	not out		14
F. Gruggen		b Day	2			
Taylor		b Day	3			
G. Gruggen		b Day	27	not out		27
Dowker		b Seaton	1			
Philips		b Seaton	5			
Young	c Botterill	b Seaton	1			
Key		b Day	5			
Morris	c Botterill	b Harrison	11	c Harrison b Burton		7
Matthews	not out		3	run out		2
Extras 5b, 2lb, 14w			21	Extras 3w		3
			104		3 for	58

DRIFFIELD: 1st Innings

W. Botterill		b Taylor	0
Seaton	c Dowker	b Phillips	0
Kirkby		b Phillips	2
Day	c Key	b Taylor	6
Matthews		b Taylor	12
Burton		b Phillips	7
A. Botterill	c Philips	b Taylor	1
Railton		b Phillips	2
Harrison	not out		7
Teal	run out		1
Packard		b Taylor	0
Extras 5b, 1lb, 7w, 1nb			14
			52

Stumps drawn at 6.00 p.m.

Pocklington won on the basis of the 1st innings.

HEDON WELLINGTON v HULL ZINGARI
Played at Hedon 14th July 1860

HEDON WELLINGTON: 1st Innings   **2nd Innings**

Player	1st dismissal	1st bowler	1st runs	2nd dismissal	2nd bowler	2nd runs
W. Kirk	c Scott	b Terry	0	c Jackson	b Terry	4
F. Foster		b Terry	0		b Scott	3
G. Harland	c Abbey	b Fearne	9	hit wkt	b Terry	7
Rev. E. Kay	run out		3		b Terry	5
Wright	c Abbey	b Bearpark	12	c Jackson	b Scott	0
Harrison	run out	Bearpark	11		b Terry	7
A. Iveson		b Bearpark	4	c Abbey	b Scott	5
J. Mould (pro)		b Bearpark	7	c Hamlyn	b Scott	2
B. Iveson		b Scott	10	not out		1
T. Johnson	c Wilde	b Bearpark	0		b Scott	3
Cpt. White	not out		4		b Scott	2
Extras			16	Extras		4
			76			43

HULL ZINGARI: 1st Innings   **2nd Innings**

Player	1st dismissal	1st bowler	1st runs	2nd dismissal	2nd bowler	2nd runs
H. Terry		b Harland	14			
C. Swinney		b Mould	0			
W. Wilde		b Harland	6			
T. Scott	run out		8	not out		2
W. Jackson		b Harland	0		b Mould	12
H. Bearpark	run out		2			
W. Abbey	not out		15			
C. Bearpark		b Mould	7			
J. Fearne	run out		0	not out		3
J. Hamlyn	run out		1			
G. Eaton	c Harrison	b Mould	12			
Extras			35	Extras		4
			100			1 for 21

Zingari won by 9 wickets.

'Run out Bearpark' sometimes denotes a direct throw on the wicket by the fielder or wicket-keeper.

Hull Zingari was a casual side in 1860, not a regular club side.

DRIFFIELD v HEDON
Played at Driffield, 28th June, 1861 Wickets pitched at 11.00
Ladies free. Gentlemen 3d. Luncheon will be provided at 1.00 pm

DRIFFIELD: 1st Innings				2nd Innings		
Seaton		b A. Iveson	4	c and b	b A. Iveson	0
W. Botterill	st	b A. Iveson	6	run out		7
Harrison	lbw	Clapham	1	c B. Iveson		
					b A. Iveson	6
Teal		b Clapham	1		b A. Iveson	3
A. Botterill	c B. Iveson	b A. Iveson	22	c Kirk	b A. Iveson	4
Day		b A. Iveson	1	run out		3
F. Matthews		b A. Iveson	4	st	b Kay	15
Burton		b A. Iveson	0	not out		1
R. Botterill	lbw	A. Iveson	0			
Fawcett	c Harland	b A. Iveson	1			
M. Matthews	not out		0			
Extras 1lb, 8w, 4b			18	Extras 3w, 3b		6
			53		7 for	45

HEDON:		1st Innings	
Kirk	lbw	b Day	2
Harland	run out		17
Kay	c Teal	b Day	0
Foster		b Harrison	0
B. Iveson	run out		12
Arth.Iveson	c B'ill	b Harrison	2
Albrt.Iveson	st B'ill	b Harrison	11
Clapham	c Day	b Harrison	0
Aug.Iveson		b Burton	8
Harland	not out		5
Bannister		b Burton	0
Extras 5lb, 4w, 13b			22
			79

UMPIRES: Mr. Escritt (Driffield) and Mr. Smith (Hedon)
Stumps drawn at 5.30.
Hedon won on the basis of the 1st Innings.

DRIFFIELD v LONDESBOROUGH
Played at Driffield, August 1862

DRIFFIELD: 1st Innings

W. Botterill	c Stephenson	b Pattinson	0
Kirkby		b Pattinson	2
Teal		b Heseltine	6
Wise	lbw	b Heseltine	3
Matthews	lbw	b Heseltine	1
A. Botterill	c Usher	b Heseltine	14
Harrison		b Heseltine	0
G. Piercey		b Heseltine	0
Railton		b Heseltine	0
Morris	st Heseltine	b Pattinson	0
Hewson	not out		0
Extras 2b, 2w, 1lb			5
			31

LONDESBOROUGH: 1st Innings

Usher		b Wise	11
Jefferson	c Harrison	b Wise	4
Hall		b Railton	0
Scott		b Railton	0
Stephenson	c A. Botterill	b Wise	8
Heseltine		b Railton	4
Wilson	c Piercey	b Wise	1
Pattinson		b Wise	1
Egerton	c Matthews	b Wise	1
Musgrave	not out		3
Scott	c and	b Wise	2
Extras 2b			2
			40

Rain prevented a second innings being played.
Londesborough won on the basis of the 1st Innings. Note Heseltine's 8 wickets and a stumping in the same innings.

HORNSEA (WADE'S) CLUB v THE INSTITUTE (HULL)
Played at Hornsea on Saturday, 5th August, 1865

HORNSEA: 1st Innings				2nd Innings		
Hore	c Reinold	b Hardy	0	c Clarke	b Wilde	1
Waltham		b Wilde	0	c and	b Wilde	0
Thomson		b Hardy	3	run out		1
Wade	c Cussons	b Hardy	24		b Reinold	5
Fern		b Wilde	9		b Reinold	0
Holmes	c Clarke	b Hardy	0		b Reinold	2
Mercer		b Reinold	10		b Wilde	2
Gibson		b Wilde	0	c Cussons	b Wilde	1
Beale	c Reinold	b Hardy	0	c Reinold	b Wilde	0
Heslop		b Wilde	2		b Reinold	0
Bennett	not out		0	not out		1
Extras			2	Extras		2
			50			15

THE INSTITUTE:		1st Innings	
Hall		b Waltham	10
Clarke	c Fern	b Waltham	1
Hardy		b Wade	0
Cussons		b Waltham	2
Wilde	run out		15
Reinold		b Wade	22
Swift	c Wade	b Waltham	14
Proctor		b Waltham	12
Walker		b Hore	8
Guy	not out		2
Gray		b Waltham	0
Extras			24
			110

The Institute won by an innings and 45 runs

174

Played at Bridlington, 14th and 15th August, 1865

BURLINGTON: 1st Innings   2nd Innings

T. Ripon		b Ferrand	0		b Carter	0
R. Baker	c. Osborne	b Freeman	3	c and	b Ferrand	1
R. Crowe		b Freeman	3		b Ferrand	4
R. Teal		b Ferrand	1		b Ferrand	9
L. Fulton		b Freeman	1	c Wright	b Osborne	1
M. Prickett		b Freeman	0	run out		4
Lyon	c Atkinson	b Freeman	4	c Carter	b Osborne	1
R. Preston	c Walker	b Ferrand	7		b Ferrand	1
H. Pease	run out		6	c and	b Ferrand	10
G. Hewson		b Ferrand	1	st Osborne	b Ferrand	0
R. Leadley	st Osborne	b Ferrand	2		b Ferrand	0
R. Bolton	c	b Smith	0	c Walker	b Ferrand	0
H. Terry	c and	b Ferrand	2		b Osborne	4
Beaupark		b Ferrand	0	c Freeman	b Osborne	0
J. Bilton		b Freeman	0		b Osborne	0
T. Duggleby		b Freeman	1		b Ferrand	1
J. Dyson		b Freeman	6		b Ferrand	5
W. Rhodes		b Ferrand	5		b Osborne	0
R. Whittaker	st Osborne	b Ferrand	0	st	b Ferrand	0
T. Prickett		b Ferrand	0		b Osborne	3
J. Wright		b Ferrand	0	run out		3
Adams	not out		0	not out		3
Extras			2	Extras		2
			39		(sic)	**48**

YORK AND DISTRICT XI: 1st Innings

G. Osborne	c Baker	b Beaupark	14
F. Walker		b Beaupark	16
E. Carter		b Beaupark	0
G. Freeman		b Terry	2
C. Penrose		b Terry	0
T. Gray	c Teal	b Terry	7
H. Ferrand	c Teal	b Hewson	26
J. Atkinson		b Beaupark	0
W. Smith	not out		24
F. Matthews		b Beaupark	6
H. Wright	c	b Fulton	0
Extras			10
			105

York won by an innings and 18 runs

HULL v MALTON
Played at Hull 1866

HULL: 1st Innings				2nd Innings		
Fawcett	run out		0	c Freeman	b Dewse	4
C. Ullathorne	c Atkinson	b Dewse	3		b Freeman	5
F. Scott		b Freeman	9	not out		15
H. Terry	c and	b Dewse	4	st Hawkins	b Dewse	29
A. Crossland	c Matthews	b Dewse	2	lbw		6
J. Greenwood	not out		8	c Freeman	b Dewse	3
J. W. Crossland	run out		1		b Dewse	1
T. Dixon	c Rose	b Dewse	0		b Dewse	4
G. Harland		b Freeman	2	run out		4
R. Carver	c Key	b Freeman	0	not out		8
Reinold		b Freeman	1			
Extras			3	Extras		2
			33		8 for	34

MALTON:		1st Innings	
J. Hawkins		b Greenwood	0
J. S. Tate		b A. Crossland	0
J. Key	run out		15
G. Freeman		b A. Crossland	10
H. Dewse	c Terry	b Greenwood	47
Rev. E.M. Cole		b A. Crossland	1
J. Wise	c and	b A. Crossland	5
F. C. Matthews	not out		15
F. Atkinson		b A. Crossland	2
W. H. Rose		b Greenwood	0
R. Boulton	c Terry	b Greenwood	1
Extras			5
			101

Malton won on the basis of the 1st Innings.
It was after this match that Terry challenged Freeman to a single wicket match.

CAPTAIN EGERTON'S XI v BRANTINGHAMTHORPE DALE
Played at Londesborough Park, August 1868

CAPT. EGERTON'S XI: 1st Innings

G. Pottage		b Clayton	0
J. Coxen		b Wilde	3
F. Milner		b Clayton	2
H. Armisted	c Fawcett	b Wilde	4
R. Egerton		b Wilde	0
E. Usher		b Clayton	4
A. Egerton		b Wilde	4
G. Milner	not out		0
Scott		b Wilde	0
G. Egerton		b Waltham	9
Cpt. Egerton	absent		
Extras			5
			31

BRANTINGHAMTHORPE DALE: 1st Innings

R. Teal		b Armisted	12
Fawcett		b Armisted	3
Shepherd	c Armisted	b Pottage	0
V. Donop		b Coxen	11
A. Beaumont		b Armisted	0
G. Hewson	c R. Egerton	b Coxen	32
Twiss		b Armisted	4
R. Waltham	st Cpt. Egerton	b Usher	8
Clayton	st Cpt. Egerton	b Usher	7
Wilde	not out		8
Fearne	c out	b Usher	0
Extras			11
			96

Not quite country-house cricket nor club cricket. Brantingham is an invitation XI consisting mainly of Driffield, Hull and Beverley players. Wilde was a professional. Egerton's XI, with its four family members, is not quite the normal Londesborough Park side. Coxen was the pro.

177

NORTH v SOUTH
Played at Hull, 9th, 10th and 11th September 1875

THE SOUTH: 1st Innings · 2nd Innings

W. R. Gilbert		b Emmett	9	run out		6
G. F. Grace		b Emmett	3		b Hill	10
C. Charlwood		b Emmett	2		b Hill	4
J. Lillywhite	c Ulyett	b Hill	5	c Emmett	b Jackson	0
W. G. Grace	c Pinder	b Emmett	29	c and	b Hill	37
H. Jupp		b Emmett	6	st Pinder	b Hill	4
R. Humphrey	c Ulyett	b Lockwood	40		b Hill	5
E. Pooley	c Jackson	b Emmett	2	st Pinder	b Jackson	8
R. Fillery		b Emmett	0	c and	b Hill	5
F. Silcock	not out		30	c and	b Jackson	12
J. Southerton	c P'er	b Emmett	3	not out		0
Extras			8	Extras		2
			137			**93**

THE NORTH: 1st Innings · 2nd Innings

A. N. Hornby	c and b Lillywhite		48	absent		
E. Lockwood	lbw	b W.G.Grace	0	c Silcock	b Southerton	9
A. Greenwood	lbw	b W.G.Grace	35	c G. Grace	b W.G.Grace	7
F. Wilde		b Southerton	0	c and	b W.G.Grace	2
G. Ulyett	c W.G.Grace	b Southerton	0		b Southerton	3
T. Emmett	run out		15		b W.G.Grace	0
C. Ullathorne	not out		26	c Gilbert	b Southerton	5
L. Jackson		b Southerton	1		b W.G.Grace	11
J. Rowbotham		b W.G.Grace	5		b W.G.Grace	21
A. Hill	c Humphrey	b W.G.Grace	10		b Southerton	1
C. Pinder	c sub	b W.G.Grace	3	not out		0
Extras			3	Extras		2
			146			**61**

The South won by 23 runs.

'Mr. Hornby's absence was much commented on.'

HULL TOWN v AUSTRALIAN ELEVEN
18th, 19th and 20th July 1878

HULL TOWN: 1st Innings				2nd Innings		
W. Rigley	c Bailey	b Spofforth	38	c Gregory	b Boyle	7
H. Taylor	c Gregory	b Moran	53	c Bannerman	b Boyle	2
A. Greenwood	c Spoff'h	b Murdoch	49		b Boyle	23
W. Clarke	st Blackham	b Spoff'h	11		b Boyle	0
L. Jackson		b Murdoch	2		b Boyle	4
L. Wallgate	c Bannerman	b Boyle	14	c and	b Boyle	8
A. Wood		b Allen	23	not out		3
D. Hearfield	c Blackham	b Boyle	2	c B'ham	b Spoff'h	2
M. McIntyre		b Murdoch	30	c B'ham	b Spoff'h	14
E.B. Rawlinson	c and	b Boyle	19	absent		
A. Smith	not out	b Emmett	1	c and	b Boyle	4
Extras			8	Extras		1
			250			68

AUSTRALIA: 1st Innings				2nd Innings
C. Bannerman	c Rigley	b McIntyre	8	not out
W. Murdoch	c Greenwood	b McIntyre	5	not out
T. Horan	c Greenwood	b Wallgate	50	
D. Gregory	run out		0	
T. Garrett		b McIntyre	10	
F. R. Spofforth	c Clarke	b Jackson	16	
G. H. Bailey	c McIntyre	b Wallgate	20	
F. A. Allan	c Clarke	b Rawlinson	78	
J. M. Blackham		b Rigley	53	
J. Conway		b Wallgate	46	
H. F. Boyle	not out		13	
Extras			6	
			305	14

Australia won by 10 wickets (but batted on)

HULL TOWN:
W. Rigley, A. Smith (Derbyshire), H. Taylor (Beverley), A. Greenwood (Yorkshire), W. Clarke (Scarborough), L. Jackson, L. Wallgate, D. Hearfield (Hull), M. McIntyre (Nottinghamshire), E. B. Rawlinson (Malton), A. Wood.

LONDESBOROUGH PARK v YORKSHIRE GENTLEMEN
Played at Londesborough, 12th June 1886

LONDESBOROUGH PARK:

W. A. Usher	c Cholmley	b Archdale	6
Boyes		b Boddy	27
J. Wreghitt	c Leatham	b Archdale	1
Goodall	c Hawke	b Archdale	12
H. Dobbinson	c Hildyard	b Archdale	2
W. Brown		b Boddy	0
A. Siddall	c Leatham	b Boddy	3
H. Usher		b Boddy	2
A. Ward		b Archdale	3
E. R. Young		b Archdale	10
G. Cobb	not out		5
Extras			5
			76

YORKSHIRE GENTLEMAN:

Cpt. Flint		b Siddall	8
G. A. B. Leatham	c H. Usher	b Goodall	6
Boddy		b Siddall	7
Cpt. Archdale	c Dobbinson	b Boyes	9
Cpt. Witherley	c Boyes	b Siddall	3
Hon. M. B. Hawke		b Siddall	10
Cpt. Seymour		b Siddall	2
G. Croft		b Siddall	1
R. G. Cholmley	not out		10
H. J. Hildyard	c and	b H. Usher	17
E. Jones		b Siddall	9
Extras			5
			87

SOUTH HOLDERNESS C.C. v HORNSEA C.C.
Played at Hedon in 1883

HORNSEA:

H. Saxelby	c Coates	b Eckroyd	4
J. W. Watson	c Foster	b Crosby	0
R. C. Bolton	c Thompson	b Crosby	2
E. F. Ingleby	c Peck	b Eckroyd	16
H. N. Wade		b Thompson	11
F. B. Moss		b Eckroyd	0
R. J. Wade	run out		0
H. W. Stork		b Thompson	2
A. W. Lambert	not out		1
J. Kerr		b Eckroyd	1
P. Everingham		b Eckroyd	0
Extras			4
			41

SOUTH HOLDERNESS:

W. E. Coates	c Stork	b Moss	2
F. Foster		b Bolton	1
T. Peck	c Stork	b H. N. Wade	24
E. Eckroyd		b Bolton	1
Rev. E. B. Kay	c Saxelby	b H. N. Wade	0
J. H. Markham	c Lambert	b H. N. Wade	0
A. B. Iveson		b H. N. Wade	7
J. K. Thompson		b Bolton	0
T. Crosby		b H. N. Wade	3
G. F. Harland	not out		1
J. Myers		b H. N. Wade	4
Extras			19
			72

1883 was the year in which South Holderness C.C. was formed. R. C. Bolton on the Hornsea side was the Yorkshire County player.

181

BRIDLINGTON AND DISTRICT XI v THE PARSEES
Played at Bridlington, 7th September 1888

THE PARSEES: 1st Innings / 2nd Innings

Batsman	1st dismissal	Runs	2nd dismissal		Runs
J. M. Morenas	b Gibson	4	st Hobson	b Burton	0
P. D. Kanga	b Garforth	59		b Burton	5
D. S. Melita	b Gibson	3	not out		19
Erance	c Burton b Garforth	6		b Gibson	4
S. O. Else	c Cooper b Garforth	2		b Burton	21
N. C. Bapasola	b Gibson	19	c Ream	b Gibson	4
D. F. Dubash	b Burton	51		b Burton	1
M. D. Kanga	b Garforth	3	c Walker	b Gibson	3
M. E. Pavri	not out	7	c Burton	b Gibson	1
S. H. Harver	b Burton	0		b Garforth	5
B. D. Moody	b Burton	3	run out		7
Extras		12	Extras		3
		169			**73**

BRIDLINGTON AND DISTRICT: 1st Innings / 2nd Innings

Batsman	1st dismissal	Runs	2nd dismissal		Runs
A. E. Gibson	b Pavri	3		b Pavri	17
R. J. Miller	b Pavri	3	c Bapasola	b Pavri	14
R. E. Walker	not out	30	c and	b P. Kanga	30
W. Dandison	c and b Pavri	11		b P. Kanga	0
Garforth	c Erance b Pavri	20		b P. Kanga	3
C. Ream	run out	1	not out		25
C. P. Sykes	b Pavri	1	c and	b Pavri	28
F. Harland	b Pavri	2		b Pavri	0
C. Whittington	c Bapasola b Pavri	2	c Bapasola	b Pavri	0
E. F. Burton	lbw	13	lbw	b Pavri	4
A. Hobson	b P.D. Kanga	0		b Pavri	0
Extras		5	Extras		10
		91			**131**

The Parsees won by 20 runs.

182

BRIDLINGTON AND DISTRICT v DUTCH TOURING ELEVEN
Played at Bridlington August 27th 1892

THE DUTCH XI:

Eyken		b Atkinson	0
Schroder		b Atkinson	0
De Haas		b Taylor	5
Posthuma		b Atkinson	5
Spranger	c W. H. Cranswick	b Hornstead	35
De Groot	c Nutt	b Atkinson	6
Moeder	lbw	b Atkinson	4
Costery	not out		23
Van Der Bosch		b Hornstead	2
Rouffuer	run out		27
Kupper	c Hornstead	b Atkinson	4
Extras			21
			132

BRIDLINGTON AND DISTRICT:

R. J. Miller		b Posthuma	5
C. A. Whittington		b De Haas	7
F. Atkinson		b Postuma	40
Joe Cranswick	c Moeder	b De Haas	10
A. Hornstead		b De Haas	0
R. Crowe	c and	Posthuma	31
J. Nutt	run out		6
W. H. Cranswick		b Posthuma	2
H. Taylor	not out		8
H. Beauvais	not out		0
Extras			0
			109

Match drawn